D0479088

# Cold Calling Is A Waste Of Time: Sales Success In The Information Age

## The *Never Cold Call Again*® System

by
Frank J. Rumbauskas Jr.
New York Times Best-Selling Author

## www.NeverColdCall.com

**E-Book ISBN # 0-9765163-1-4**
**Print Book ISBN # 0-9765163-0-6**

## All-New 7th Edition, 2013

## To learn more, to subscribe to Frank's free newsletter, learn about Frank's other books, speaking, and more, please visit:

## www.NeverColdCall.com

Frank is available to teach *your* sales team how to never cold call again, and explode their sales numbers in the process!

For more information on live sales training, or to have Frank speak at your next event, please contact Ashley at:

ashley@nevercoldcall.com

# Table of Contents

## Part 4:
## The *Never Cold Call Again*® Social Media Selling System

## Part 5:
## The Never Cold Call Again® Advanced Referral Selling Strategies

## Part 6:
## Take Action Now!

# Foreword
# By Jeff McElroy

Over the course of my career I have sold copiers, business telephone systems, IT networks and equipment, wireless internet services, telecom services, and presently I am prospering in the life insurance business. As you can see, my background is quite diverse and includes both business-to-business and business-to-consumer sales.

This prospecting system works for all of them, and it will work for you, but ONLY if you put it into action.

I first met Frank Rumbauskas over six years ago when I was an owner in a wireless internet company, and Frank was on our sales force. We had five account executives in the office, yet Frank consistently contributed over 50% of the total sales production. You read that right - he was one out of five sales reps, yet he sold more than HALF the total sales production in the company!

Here's the twist: Frank did this while rarely working an entire day, and most days he worked only five hours or so. The other reps who couldn't come close to him in production worked full eight-hour days, and frequently longer than that. While they were staying late trying to catch up and make sales, Frank was already home relaxing by his pool.

He was able to do this using the techniques explained in this book. I know this because I was his boss at the time and I saw him do it firsthand. Why did those other reps have to work so hard to sell less than Frank? I know the answer to that question too. It's because they spent their time working hard at cold calling instead of working smart like Frank did.

When I got into the life insurance business as an agent a few years ago, I used Frank's system as presented in this book to immediately begin making five figures per month without cold calling. Not long after I formed an agency of my own, recruited agents, and trained them using Frank's system combined with my own experience in selling insurance. Frank's proven system is working once again for all of us.

Remember when I said this will work ONLY if you put it into action? The agents who put the system into action are prospering. Those who didn't are no longer with us. Why? Because this system works, and all the old outdated sales techniques you've probably been taught don't. Especially cold calling.

If you use this system, you will enjoy the success I've achieved, the success my agents have achieved, and the success that thousands of Frank's readers are achieving. Remember, it all comes down to you and whether or not you put the system into action. The choice is yours. Implement these techniques, and you will be a top producer almost immediately.

Jeff McElroy, President
JD McElroy Financial Advisors

# Preface
## by Frank Rumbauskas

When I wrote the first edition of *Cold Calling Is A Waste Of Time* in 2003, I had no idea it would take off the way it did. This book-and-CD package literally became an overnight sensation, and has since gone through many changes and additions, evolving into the *Never Cold Call Again*® system today. This system has become popular all over the world simply because it works.

When I wrote the first edition and put up the website, I was hoping I might sell a copy here and there and make a few hundred dollars a month on the side. I was happy at my job and doing very well, yet little did I know I would quit less than two months later to become a full-time author, speaker, and consultant.

What really baffled me, though, was the fact that no one else had previously written a book explaining these techniques on how to sell without cold calling. I knew for a fact that other top-performing salespeople were using many of these principles (very few salespeople, but nevertheless others were using them), and I'd assumed that there must be another book or course outlining these tactics already on the market.

I was wrong, and to this day, I'm still shocked to see no one else teaching this material. Apparently the old-school world of selling, notorious for its orders of "cold call more" and "increase your activity," has got a death grip on everyone.

After releasing the first edition and experiencing such quick and sudden success, I felt a little bit guilty. After all, I was enjoying all that success without having to work much. I built a business to sell this book, set up an automated system to accomplish that, and sat back and enjoyed the passive income. Something within me changed, though, after I began to receive dozens, then hundreds, and eventually thousands of letters and e-mails from salespeople who had begun using my system with great success.

Something about hearing from a single mom who had doubled her income, or from a rookie who finally "got it" and started making money, or from a dad who was able to suddenly work less and spend more time with his kids, touched me inside and made me realize that this isn't just my source of income – it's now my mission.

With that in mind I've expanded my efforts to teach salespeople to stop cold calling forever. I've accomplished a lot to that end over the past nine years, and now I'm proudly releasing this sixth edition of Cold Calling Is A Waste Of Time, which includes much additional knowledge I've gained over these past few years, including a lot of great new Information Age selling tools including social media.

I've gotten to know several other authors recently, and in the process I've learned that we all share the same frustration. That frustration is the terrible habit most people have of reading a book, then putting it down and never doing anything about it again. I'd say well over ninety percent of my readers probably read this, say "Wow, that was interesting, I guess I really could stop cold calling and sell more in the end," then they never implement any of the techniques. I also know from contact with readers that most of the ones who do decide to take action put one or two of my tactics into use, but that's it. They never try them all, and never build the system of systems I'll explain later on. So, it was no surprise to me to learn that nearly every other sales and self-improvement author has the same frustration.  If we had just one wish, it would be to have our readers actually use what we teach!

So, with that in mind, I'll stop there and let you dig into the book.  Remember, it's all useless if you don't use it, so I hope you will!  Because when you do, you'll be in that top one percent of top producers that all salespeople only wish they could join!

Frank J. Rumbauskas Jr.
May, 2012

## Part 1: A Background on Cold Calling & Lead Generation

# Introduction

"Oh no, I haven't failed 5,000 times.  I've succeeded
in finding 5,000 different ways that you cannot possibly
build a light bulb."

- Thomas A. Edison,
on his progress during his quest for the
*incandescent electric lamp*

Cold calling is a waste of time.

Those words generate quite a variety of responses from different salespeople at different places in their respective careers.  The most common reactions I hear are as follows:

- "Wow, somebody else gets it!  It's nice to see the truth finally coming out in the mainstream media."
  - Successful salespeople in our new Information Age economy

- "You know, I've always thought so myself.  It seems like I bang my head against the wall cold calling but not much ever seems to come from it."
  - The majority of salespeople

- "Are you kidding me?  That's just a lazy attitude.  You've got to beat the streets, knock doors, pound the pavement, and dial for dollars every day, day in and day out, if you can possibly have any success in sales.  There's no other way to do it.  There are no tricks, scams, or anything else you can do other than hard work."
  - The 'old timers' out there, most of whom are burned out

- "We require our salespeople to do 50 cold calls per day.  They must document this with call logs if it's on the phone or with business cards if they're going out in person."
  - The vast majority of unsuccessful sales managers

The sad reality is that cold calling is generally accepted, endorsed, and even forced upon salespeople by the vast majority of books, training materials, corporate training programs, and managers, despite the fact that it stopped producing any appreciable results years ago.

In 1989, the Berlin Wall fell, marking the end of communism in that part of the world.  This significant event in world history is considered by many to mark the end of our old Industrial Age economy and the beginning of our new Information Age economy.  Computers and electronics began to advance in even larger leaps and bounds than before and shortly thereafter the Internet came to be and changed the way we communicate and do business in ways that nobody ever imagined. What's more, the Internet and other Information Age technologies that haven't even been invented yet will continue to change our world in ways that most of us cannot possibly imagine today.

In spite of all this, the world of outside selling clings to old beliefs and methods that go back to the turn of the 20$^{th}$ century. Every other aspect of the business world has changed dramatically and quickly but most sales departments still advocate and even require "beating the streets," "dialing for dollars," "pounding the pavement," and a host of other clichés that are regularly used to describe what's underneath it all – cold calling. To make the situation worse, many companies and managers require salespeople to waste vast amounts of time cold calling through micro-management, requiring documentation of cold calling in the form of call logs and business cards, and block out massive amounts of productive selling time to carry out "blitzes."

If you're reading this book, you know cold calling doesn't work. It has failed you. The purpose of this book, the associated audio program, and the classes and seminars we teach is to show salespeople a better way to prospect and attract pre-qualified customers who are ready, willing, and even eager to buy from you immediately.

You'll need to keep an open mind as you learn this material. A portion of this program is devoted to what seems like "bashing" the concept of cold calling and anyone who advocates it as a legitimate method of prospecting for business. The reason for this is because you need to know in your heart and mind that it's obsolete before your subconscious can be ready and willing to accept and work on the ideas we're going to show you. A lot of salespeople we've worked with like what we had to say, but managed to get by every month by spending long hours doing intensive cold calling, and instead of putting our program into action, they stuck with the "safe and secure" methods they've been using for so long instead of moving into the Information Age and increasing their results exponentially.

Take the attitude of Thomas A. Edison. Instead of becoming frustrated with selling and thinking that you've failed to do the things that work, realize that you've been successful in finding things that don't work. Once you find all the things that don't work, all that's left are the things that work. That's what you're going to learn and that's what's in store for you.

Keep an open mind as you read this book and listen to the CDs. Some of our techniques seem overly simple and you may think they're too obvious to actually work. That isn't true. They work. On the other hand, some of this may seem a bit complex. Don't worry about that. Immediately start putting the simpler techniques into action and gradually work up to the more complex ones. You WILL see results. You WILL succeed!

# My Story

"Cold calling is a waste of time!"

- Frank Rumbauskas,
sick and tired of spending 12-hour
days cold calling to no avail

Let me tell you my personal story because my definition and interpretation of selling has changed so many times and in so many ways during my years of sales experience. You may find that my personal experience parallels your own.

My very first direct selling experience was in my early teens when a friend and I became deeply interested in ham radio and started going to swap meets, or "hamfests" as they're called, on weekends. Like most kids at that age, we were fascinated by anything new and started buying old ham radio equipment, typically for about five to ten bucks a radio, and soon had a nice little collection going. Naturally we started checking out the classifieds in "QST," which is the national ham radio magazine, and much to our surprise, some of these same radios we were buying for five bucks apiece sold for a hundred dollars in the national classifieds. We didn't realize it at the time but very few cities offer the sheer volume of hamfests that the NYC area offers, and even back in Phoenix where I lived for many years, the nation's fifth-largest city, we only had a few each year. Naturally the law of supply-and-demand kicks in and hams out in rural areas were willing to pay big bucks for radios that were readily available to us for a few dollars each (I say "were" because eBay has since ruined all the fun). So guess what we did? We started running classifieds and soon were making a nice profit of about ninety bucks on every radio we sold, and in some months we sold a lot. What I would do is buy 10 of the same model radio for five dollars each, run a classified ad advertising the same radio for $100, and sell one to each of the first 10 people who called. We were laughing all the way to the bank and having a blast while most of our friends were working crummy summer jobs for minimum wage! To a 14-year old kid, making a thousand dollars a month without working was pretty amazing and I'm still proud of it today. This early experience formed the basis in my mind of what selling is, how it should be, and the concept of working smart, not hard. It also showed me that hard work isn't necessary to make a lot of money, and seeing my friends sweep floors for a few bucks an hour taught me that working hard for a paycheck is actually counter-productive and not very intelligent. That's how my interest in commission sales started.

Not long after, I took an interest in politics and found myself volunteering to work for a presidential campaign at the age of 15. It was a great way to make friends and meet new people, and that continues to be the case in my life today. Anyway, volunteering consisted of mundane office tasks, stuffing envelopes, and working the phone banks. I wasn't looking forward to working the phones and was actually intimidated at first but found it to be quite easy, and even had several people tell me they're changing their vote thanks to some of the arguments I made on the phone. Not bad! The campaign came to a close, we won, I had the excitement of meeting the new president, and all was well with the world.

Like most teenagers, I wanted spending money and started to gradually lose interest in the ham radio thing. I looked in the paper to find a ton of telemarketing jobs. I figured I was great at it in the campaign so I'd give it a shot. Sure enough, I was quickly making a killing working the phones for a fundraising organization that ran anti-drug campaigns targeted at kids. Our commission rate was somewhere around 10% and I'd typically get about $1,000 in donations in a 4-hour nightly shift... a cool $25/hour. It was much, much better than what all of my friends were doing at their crummy jobs and a lot easier too. Again, the concept of working smart, not hard became more concrete in my mind and a basic part of my thinking.

I'd like to mention that somewhere along the line I worked for one summer at an insurance agency. I was good with computers and frequently played around with their system looking for ways to automate and simplify my tasks (back to the "work smart, not hard" rule). Unfortunately, one of the owners was NOT very computer literate, interpreted my never-ending exploring within their computer system as hacking, and unfairly fired me. This event is important because it forced me to realize at an early age that a regular 8-5 job would never bring me any happiness or satisfaction and that I'd need to focus my efforts in life on finding ways to be efficient and innovative rather than working long hours for a fixed paycheck. It also helped me to learn that working for someone else only benefits whoever that someone else is and does nothing for me.

College came and went rather quickly. I never liked school and my intense hatred for structure and authority really shined through. I was thrown off campus for using fireworks on campus and chose not to return to school the following year. At the time it seemed like a disaster (from a young age I was brainwashed that not going to college meant certain poverty) but looking back, it's probably the best thing that happened to me. If I stayed I would have ended up working as an engineer with a massive student loan debt to repay. Even if that happened I'm sure I would've gotten sick of it pretty quickly and ended up in sales anyway! To this day, people occasionally ask me if I intend to get a degree, to which my reply is, "Why? So I can spend four years and an obscene amount of money only to come back to doing the same kind of work?" Don't get me wrong, I have nothing against college and when I eventually have kids I'd like them to go, but it's not necessary for sales like it is for a career in medicine, teaching, law, etc. In fact, many top salespeople never completed college, or even high school for that matter, and make more money than the top doctors and lawyers in our society. Not to mention the fact that their job is a lot less stressful!

All teenage boys love cars and I was no exception, so that parlayed into a job as an auto mechanic for a year. Tired of coming home every night with grease all over my arms, transmission fluid in my hair and cuts on my hands, not to mention a lousy paycheck, I decided it was time to get back to sales. Having had no outside sales experience, I quickly found my way back to the telemarketing world, this time a "real" job with Dun & Bradstreet selling credit service subscriptions to small business owners nationwide. Once again I excelled on the phones. It was also the first time I was required to dress up and wear a tie every day and I loved the attention it brought me. I somewhat regretted having a girlfriend at the time because wearing nice clothes opened up a whole new world of single women! I'm guessing it's that experience that turned me into something of a clothes fanatic who chooses to wear suits in the 120-degree Phoenix weather, eliciting looks of disbelief from passerby. It was also my first job in a truly corporate setting, which I liked as well. As a kid on summer vacation I loved going to work with my father at Western Electric, which eventually became AT&T and then Lucent Technologies. The funny thing about it is how cute everyone thought it was when I'd say, "I want to work here when I grow up," and eventually I did! In any case, I felt quite comfortable in a corporate setting and that shaped some of my later career decisions.

So here I was, loving my job at D&B, making decent money, but alas, plans changed and that came to a sudden end. My girlfriend's father had just moved to Hawaii. She and I already knew we didn't want to stay in New Jersey but had no clue as to where to go. Her dad was bugging someone to come out there so we went for it. We moved, stayed with him for a few weeks until we got a place, and that was that. Little did I know at the time that the Big Island of Hawaii had 20% unemployment and practically no economy outside of tourism and the coffee and sugar farms, so it wasn't long before I was desperate for work. I took a job in a Salvation Army store for seven bucks an hour until something better came along, which did in the form of a radio station. The top station on the island had just brought in a new sales manager, Mason, who was a sharp and exceptionally friendly guy. Despite my lack of outside selling experience and total ignorance of the radio and advertising world, he gave me a shot and hired me. I quickly learned that the phone isn't a welcome way of selling in Hawaii so I got my first experience at "pounding the pavement" - door-to-door cold calling. Things went okay for a while, I struggled, sold some accounts, and eventually became frustrated. After my recoverable draw finally ran out I wasn't making enough to survive on commission alone so I regretfully left and soon found myself on a car lot.

Hawaii Motors was a bit unusual for a car dealership. I lived in Kailua-Kona, a small town on the west side of the Big Island of Hawaii. With a population of only about 40,000, there wasn't enough of a market to support numerous auto dealerships, so there were a few big ones instead. We were a GM dealer and sold every one of GM's makes on our lot, including both new and used cars. I got my first sale the third day on the job, a new GMC pickup, and almost fainted when the boss handed me my commission voucher for the sale - $1,500. I had no idea I'd make so much on each deal! I subsequently learned that $1,500 is on the high side for a sale but the money was good nevertheless. I didn't like the job much due to the enormous pressure to sell and the fact that I was stuck on the lot for 12 hours every day with no freedom to leave, but I stayed there for the remainder of my time in Hawaii. One of the frustrations had to do with the fact that car salesmen are paid a percentage of gross profit on each deal, and for that reason we made a lot more money by selling a used car instead of a new one. However, the dealer needs to move new cars and has a quota assigned by the manufacturer and so we were under constant pressure to sell new, not used, even though the average commission on a used car was about a thousand dollars compared to one or two hundred for a new car. This was the first in a long series of experiences working for companies that have lopsided and unfair policies in place that, if corrected, would drastically increase sales production and make life a whole lot easier for everyone involved.

As beautiful as Hawaii was, after a year and a half my girlfriend and I were getting bored and had had enough of the outrageous taxes and working at jobs we didn't particularly like. Las Vegas was the big craze at the time and it seemed like all of Hawaii was moving there so we jumped on the bandwagon and made the move too. Before going, I obtained a Vegas phone book. I knew selling cars wasn't for me and that I wanted to be in outside sales, preferably in a corporate setting. Rather than send out the usual mundane resume, I created a bold tri-fold brochure entitled "Frank Rumbauskas - Sales Pro" and sent them out to every major corporation with a sales office in Las Vegas. The response was surprisingly good and I was able to schedule several interviews in advance of moving (we were too broke to travel back and forth to interview ahead of time). I had three offers within a week of arrival and quickly accepted a position with Sprint. A week later I was shipped off to new-hire training and subsequently remained in the telecom industry for several years.

Sprint was a tough job. I was a small business sales rep for Sprint long-distance at a time when the long-distance boom was coming to an end and business owners were fed up with getting ten sales calls a day. I cold called endlessly, both on foot and on the phone. I was soon known as the "cold calling monster" around the office and was admired for my work ethic and persistence, but there was a strange circumstance in the fact that I had very few sales to show for all my hard work and long days of sweating out in the desert heat to hit 50 or 60 doors. I soon found myself on probation. First a verbal warning, then a written warning, and eventually the final written warning. By this time I had 30 days to either make my numbers or get fired. Because Sprint's training taught me to cold call for business, I had no idea how to get out of the jam I was in. Instead of the shame of being fired and the fact that I wouldn't be eligible for re-hire, I submitted my two-week notice and went out looking for another job. This turned out to be a smart move because I eventually returned to Sprint a few years later which wouldn't have been possible if I had been fired and therefore red-flagged as "not eligible for re-hire."

I quickly received an offer from another large long-distance company, Bernie Ebbers' infamous WorldCom, and was back to work immediately. Because I was starting to know more people in town, I managed to sell a little bit more than I did at Sprint, but still didn't find real success and didn't make the numbers necessary to keep my employment for the long haul. Eight months later, I was facing another "Final Written Warning" and once again I was a full-time job seeker.

It became very clear to me at both of those jobs that the heyday of selling long-distance was over and I needed to find something different. Remember my brief mention of going to work with my father at Western Electric and saying I wanted to work there someday? Lucent Technologies had a classified ad in the paper advertising an opening for an entry-level account executive in the Las Vegas office. At the time I had already left my second long-distance job and was working part-time as a telemarketer, which didn't pay much but I managed to get by and survive until something better came along. It was a good thing because Lucent's hiring process was very long. First an evening group interview with the entire office (a nicely catered event, if I may say so myself). Then an invitation back for a second interview. Then a standardized written test. After hearing nothing for almost two months and assuming I wasn't chosen for the job, I received a call from a human resources representative late on a Friday afternoon to offer me the position and informing me that I would be on a plane that coming Sunday afternoon for three weeks of new hire training.

The training was extremely intensive. It went from 8am to 6pm every day for three weeks. Something in that training really stood out in my mind. We really didn't cover prospecting because prior outside sales experience was a prerequisite for the job and it was assumed that everyone knew how to prospect in their own way, but when the subject of cold calling came up, the trainer had an opinion that surprised me. He said, "Cold calling doesn't work anymore. It's a waste of your time and your prospect's. Ten or fifteen years ago you could go out cold calling and people would invite you in for a cup of coffee and appreciate the information. Those days are long gone. Nowadays cold calling will get you thrown out and will be a waste of your valuable time."

This blew me away because, even though I was starting to figure out on my own that cold calling is a waste of time, it was very reassuring to hear it coming from a professional sales trainer. The irony, of course, is that he never told us what DOES work and so everyone went back to their old ways of doing things, myself included. I came out of training and spent the first few months at that job trying to scrape up business and getting that empty feeling in my stomach that another series of warnings would eventually present themselves and that I'd be out on the job market again.

To the credit of Lucent Technologies at that time, they were one of the only companies I've ever worked for that had a marketing program in place for the purpose of providing qualified leads to the salespeople. Unfortunately, we never got enough leads to make our numbers and in some months we got none whatsoever, but it was better than what I was used to by this time. I was continuing my endless cold calling and found a lead here and there, but it didn't add up to much, and even combined with the few company leads I got, it still didn't add up to enough to make my numbers on a consistent basis.

One day, I took a senior account executive out to a lead I had found that was too big for me to handle (I was an entry-level rep and was strictly limited as to what I was allowed to sell). In the car on the way over he said, "You're going about your prospecting all wrong." When I asked him what he meant, he said, "The key to success in this job is to first realize that a certain percentage of the market is pre-disposed, ready, and willing to buy your product. Instead of wasting time cold calling a bunch of people who will NEVER buy your product, you need to find and perfect ways and means of attracting the people who WANT to buy your product before they call your competitors and buy from them instead."

That simple insight changed my entire selling career. Ever since that day, I've worked on figuring out simple, cost-effective ways to do just that. Within a few months I was the top salesperson among the entry-level reps in our office, and by my sixth month of employment I won a trip to Lake Tahoe for the huge numbers I was producing.

Since that time, I've continued to perfect my methods, finding others along the way and adding them to my system, and dropping the ones that weren't producing as well as others. After years of trial and error method, I began to teach my system to others. Nearly all of them were skeptical at first and said things like "this is too simple to work" or "these things are too obvious, it's too good to be true," but the ones who kept an open mind and consistently used these techniques have gone on to great success in selling, have received promotions to management positions, and even started their own successful businesses as I have.

I'll reiterate throughout this program the importance of keeping an open mind and believing that this will work for you. If you do, you'll experience the success that myself and others have through the use of this system.

# Why Cold Calling Doesn't Work Anymore

*"When the rate of change outside exceeds
the rate of change inside, the end is in sight."*

*- Jack Welch*

Before you can be ready to understand and use the system outlined in this book, you need to understand exactly why cold calling doesn't work. Chances are you already know that it doesn't work, but may be skeptical or still clinging to cold calling because it's all you've ever been taught or because it's "safe and secure." With that in mind, let's take a look at the specific reasons why cold calling doesn't work:

## Cold calling destroys your status as a business equal

One of the things I've learned along the way is that in order to be supremely successful in the world of selling and to maintain a very high closing ratio, you need to project a very strong image that you do not need that particular customer's business and are ready and willing to walk away at any time. However, does making a cold call present the perception that you don't need their business? Of course not! When a prospect receives a cold call from you, it's VERY CLEAR that you need their business. To make matters worse, the perception out there is that important people with busy schedules don't cold call and don't have the time to cold call because they have more important things to do.

Have you ever noticed how high-producing salespeople, most notably top realtors, have their offices, letterhead, business cards, etc., highly decorated with their achievements and awards? It's impossible to step into the office or cubicle of a top producer without noticing all the plaques, certificates, and trophies displayed on the wall. You cannot correspond with one of them without noticing "President's Club," "Golden Circle," "Million Dollar Roundtable," or some other such tagline in bold print on their business cards and letterhead. Why do they do this? Is it due to arrogance? No! They do it because prospects see it, recognize this person as someone who is not desperate and does not need their business, and they automatically WANT TO BUY FROM THEM! This is the same reason why so many prospects will call into an office and immediately ask to speak with a sales manager or with the top salesperson in the office.

Cold calling creates the perception that you have nothing better to do at that particular moment than to try and scrape up business. It comes off as needy and desperate.

## Cold calling limits production and wastes valuable time

One of the key differences between successful people and organizations back in the "Industrial Age" and the successful ones in today's "Information Age" is that the successful people and companies today are using the power of **leverage** to their advantage.

Although leverage is a topic that will be covered later in this book, understand that cold calling allows you to be in only one place at one time. In other words, you are only one person and can make only one phone call or walk into only one door at a time. The results you can produce are strictly finite and are severely limited by your time and how well you are able to manage that time. On the other hand, **leveraging** the power of **systems** to work in your favor allows you to virtually be in many places at one time. While cold calling gets your message to only one person at a time (if you're lucky enough to get through to someone in the first place), the proper use of *leveraged systems* gets your message out to a tremendous number of people at one time with little or no effort on your part. You create the system, put it into place, put it to work, and it then runs itself and automatically generates leads for you.

Here's the classic example of the non-leveraged, non-systematic method of activity planning usually taught to salespeople, even in this day and age:

"Take your quota and divide it by your average dollar amount per sale to determine how many sales you need each month. Now multiply that number by the number of proposals and/or presentations you need to make to get one sale. Multiply that number by the number of appointments it typically takes you to get to the proposal stage, and multiply that by the number of cold calls it takes you to set an appointment. You now know how many cold you must do every month. Divide by twenty, and you now know what your minimum daily activity in cold calling needs to be."

Although this method contains a number of fatal flaws that will be covered later, the main and most obvious one is that it limits your production. If the total number of cold calls required exceeds the amount of free time available for cold calling, you're screwed. There are only so many selling hours in a day. Although you can't add time, you can exponentially increase your lead-generation efforts through the power of leverage, thereby beating old Father Time at his own game.

## Cold calling makes timing work against you, not for you

It doesn't do you any good to spend time with a prospect who:

- Has no need for your product
- Will buy your product in the distant future but not anytime soon
- Is already a customer
- Has just bought from your competition

This is where the issue of timing comes into play. Timing is critical in selling. As I just mentioned, there's no point in calling on someone who is not in a buying mode for your product or who has no need for it in the first place. However, cold calling forces you to spend your valuable, productive selling time with exactly these kinds of people. In order to understand the perspective of a prospect who isn't in a buying mode for your product and just received a cold call for it, let's look at some examples:

- You're going about your day when a doctor calls and says, "Hi, this is Dr. So-and-so. I'm calling today to find out when you might be available to come in for an appointment for the purpose of treating any illness we may find that you have at this time."

- You're buried under a pile of work, stressed out and falling behind a deadline when someone comes barging into your office and says, "Hi, I'm with ABC Auto Shop. We'd like to set up a time for you to bring your car into our shop so we can take a look at it and determine if there might be any reason for you to become our customer."

Stop laughing. Yes, these examples are a bit far-fetched. Yes, they sound funny and ridiculous. But guess what? This is *exactly* what the *vast majority* of prospects think when they get your cold call. When I was out cold calling for telephone systems, I never thought of the fact that most businesses buy a new one, on average, every seven to ten years. In spite of this fact, business owners typically get several calls every week from a telephone salesman trying to "set a time to come by and determine if you may have some needs we can serve." This is absurd. It makes no sense. It's counter-productive. Sure, I found a few leads this way, but it was something along the lines of one *qualified* lead for every 200 or 300 cold calls. Emphasis is on the word qualified. Read on to find out why.

## Cold calling fails to find the pre-qualified, quality leads we all want

Have you ever noticed how the conversion and closing rate for leads generated as a result of cold calling is always, without exception, drastically lower than the closing rate for leads from every other source? Call-ins, company-generated leads, responses from mailers, referrals, introductions via networking, etc. etc., ALWAYS prove to be far more valuable than leads found via cold calling. Here are some reasons why this is so:

- A large percentage of qualified buyers don't take cold calls and don't meet with salespeople unless they requested the meeting themselves. Who does this leave for the cold-call generated appointments? That's right – the time wasters who stroke you and tell you how great everything sounds, then never make a decision, never buy, or worst case, promise you the world then never return another phone call.

- When you uncover a prospect who is in a buying cycle for your product via cold calling, chances are they already have three or four competitive quotes and you're way too late in the game. To make matters worse, remember the concept of how cold calling destroys your status as a business equal? Chances are, the prospect called your competitors for quotes, not the other way around, and you're seen as the desperate one who needs the business to survive.

I'd like to touch on something that I've learned recently, and that I think is extremely important to understand in order to fully accept the fact that cold calling fails to find the really great, qualified, ready-to-buy prospects that most of us would kill for, and why it usually results in lots of flaky prospects who tell us everything we want to hear but don't buy anything in the end.

This realization came to me while I was reading an article about social dynamics, written by someone who has studied human social interaction for years. The writer was trying to explain why those who appear very cold and unapproachable in social settings do so. He explained that the standoffish personality was nothing more than a social "mask" put forth by the person for protection. Protection against what? Protection against being seduced, falling in love, etc. The writer went on to explain that those who put on a cold, unapproachable social mask are really afraid of the fact that they are extremely vulnerable to getting too close to others too fast.

The kicker came when the writer used an analogy to help explain his point. He made the following statement which was a real eye-opener for me:

"Most experienced salespeople have learned that those prospects who won't take cold calls and have giant NO SOLICITING signs plastered all over their doors are usually the easiest to sell to once you get in front of them. The reason for this is because they are actually *afraid* of salespeople. They know that their ability to resist a sales pitch is very low, and as a result, they usually buy whenever they're confronted with salespeople. On the other hand, those who willingly take cold calls on a regular basis can do so because they have a very high level of resistance to sales pitches. They know very well they're not going to buy, and so they have no fear of salespeople."

Did you get the message there? If not, read it again! This is EXACTLY why cold calling does a terrible job of getting us in front of those prime, willing, ready-to-buy prospects. They're terrified of us, and as a result they won't take our cold calls!

As time goes on I get more and more letters and emails from salespeople asking for help with flaky prospects. What I keep hearing is that prospects are getting flakier as time goes on. It's because most salespeople cold call, and those are the prospects you'll get as a result of cold calling. They're notorious for readily accepting an appointment, telling you, "Wow, that sounds great," then never returning another phone call or email again. It's because they never had any real need or intent to buy. The only way to get to those prime prospects who are easily sold is to avoid cold calling and to use other, more creative ways to get your message across to them.

## Cold calling automatically puts you in a negative light

If there's one thing that infuriates a busy, successful person, it's wasting or otherwise being disrespectful of that person's time. Guess what? There's no better way of doing this than a cold call.

Imagine you're a busy executive with a to-do list a mile long and four meetings that day. As you're juggling tasks and trying to imagine how you'll ever get out of there before 8pm, you pick up your phone to hear this: "Hi, this is Frank Rumbauskas with FJR Advisors, and I'd like to get together with you. How about Wednesday morning or Thursday afternoon? Which would be the better time for you?" Or let's say you're a consumer who just got home from a long day at work and you're sitting down to eat dinner. The phone rings, you answer it, and hear this: "Hi, this is Frank, how are you doing this evening? Is this a good time to talk for a few minutes? If not, I'll call back. What I'd really like to do is set a time we could get together and chat about your selling and what we can do to help."

Obviously, that's extremely annoying and disrespectful, and that's exactly what cold calling will accomplish better than all other methods combined. Why get on the bad side of someone who otherwise might have actually bought from you?

## Cold calling might get you into trouble with the law

I won't go into this in great detail here because laws vary from state-to-state and country-to-country, but in my home state and many others, laws have been passed banning telemarketing and all other forms of telephone cold calling. Certain businesses are exempt but are still required to file for exempt status with the state. Many states and municipalities have laws on the books making it illegal to violate a "no soliciting" sign and I have personally been face-to-face with the police and narrowly avoided arrest on one occasion. The fact that these laws exist only proves just how intrusive and disruptive cold calling really is. As if that's not enough, the U.S. now has the national "Do Not Call" law, and that's just the beginning.

## Salespeople detest cold calling!

Personally, I think this is the most significant reason why cold calling doesn't work. It's a known fact of human psychology that almost no one can have any hope of succeeding at a job they hate. Why, then, would you choose to doom yourself to failure by doing something you hate? Even the most goofy, rah-rah, new-age sales trainers and managers will readily admit that all salespeople hate calling and anyone who claims otherwise is probably lying.

# Buying vs. Selling:
# Why they aren't the same

"*Buy:*  To acquire in exchange for money or its equivalent; purchase.
*Sell:*  To exchange or deliver for money or its equivalent."

*- The Dictionary*

Now that the dictionary definitions of the words "buy" and "sell" have been shown to you, let me share with you MY definitions of buying and selling:

Buying:  The act of *willingly* acquiring for money something that you *want* or *need*.  The buyer generally leaves the transaction feeling happy and satisfied.

Selling:  Attempting to *convince* another that they want or need your product or service despite the fact that they may not.  The purchaser typically leaves the transaction with a strong feeling of "buyer's remorse."

Can you see where I'm going with this?  Let's take it a step further.  In my experience, I've come to the conclusion that *cold calling* definitely equates to my definition of *selling*.  On the other hand, using leveraged systems to attract qualified prospects to you causes my definition of *buying* to take place.  Can you see why *buying* and *selling* can never possibly take place in the same transaction and are in fact opposites of each other?  Do you also understand the meaning of the words "causes to take place?"  It means that the proper circumstances were presented to the buyer, which induced the buyer to buy from you.  That concept flies directly in the face of *selling* as I define it and its synonym *cold calling*.

Let's take a rare example where cold calling actually did result in a sale, thereby fulfilling my definition of *selling*.  The typical series of events are as follows:

1.  The customer receives a cold call from a salesperson.  After some coercion on the part of the salesperson, or perhaps several call backs, voicemail messages, and rescheduling, a firm appointment is finally set.

2.  A first appointment takes place.  The customer is automatically resistant because they naturally assume a high-pressure sales presentation will take place and so they're on guard.

3.  A secondary appointment takes place for the purpose of presenting a proposal to the customer.  The customer's sales resistance and mistrust is at an even higher level because a presentation and several attempts at "closing" are no longer a mere possibility, they're a certainty.

4.  After the presentation, the customer advises the salesperson of what the decision process is, what must take place, who must review the proposal, etc.  Instead of being patient and having the confidence of knowing he or she has tons of other deals in the works, the salesperson jumps the gun and starts calling the customer and leaving messages once or twice a week with the empty message of "I'm just calling to find out if you've made a

decision yet." The customer takes this as in insult to their intelligence because they obviously would have called if a decision to buy had taken place.

5. The customer makes the decision to buy, paperwork is signed, and installation or delivery is scheduled. The customer can't help but wonder if they might have gotten a better deal elsewhere and that they should have called around instead of buying from someone who walked in off the street, cold.

Can you see the negative theme that follows throughout the entire process? By contrast, let's take a look at the series of events constituting my definition of *buying:*

1. The customer is contacted by one of the many methods being employed by the salesperson in his or her "mini-marketing program" learned from this book. The customer recognizes the product or service advertised as something they happen to need and the customer makes the initial call. (IMPORTANT NOTE: The customer's frame of mind is set at this time and this frame carries throughout the entire sales process. When they call you, THEY are automatically placed in the position of one who NEEDS something, and YOU are automatically in the position of one who can GIVE them what they need. Conversely, when you make a cold call, YOU are the one in need and THEY are the one in a position to GIVE you what you need. See the difference? Having them call you shifts all the power right from the very beginning, something we'll discuss in more detail later.)

2. After asking some qualifying questions to make sure this person isn't a time-waster or "paper collector," the salesperson *agrees* to visit with the customer *at a time convenient to the salesperson.* (Again, notice how the customer must gain the salesperson's agreement, not the other way around as is the case with cold calling.)

3. The initial appointment takes place. The customer is eager to get this particular need fulfilled and obviously very clearly knows what the meeting is about in advance, and so the salesperson (who happens to look like a million bucks and is dressed impeccably, giving off an aura of prosperity) simply sits back and listens and asks any questions that may be appropriate. The customer is doing all the work and freely giving the salesperson all the necessary information to develop a complete, relevant proposal. The salesperson may ask some more qualifying questions at this time, possibly even irrelevant ones. (Doing so further reinforces the customer's frame of mind that they must meet certain requirements to become that salesperson's customer, not the other way around.)

4. The salesperson returns with a proposal and contracts. Because the customer eagerly *wants* and *needs* whatever is being proposed, all necessary decision makers were made aware of the meeting in advance and are present. Price objections do not take place because the salesperson effectively qualified them out right from the very start. Contracts are signed and installation or delivery is scheduled.

5. The customer walks away from the meeting happy and excited to soon receive their new product. They mention the purchase to a few other people who become curious and ask for the salesperson's card as well.

Notice how much easier the second example is for the salesperson involved. By sharp contrast, the first example sounds difficult, stressful, and negative. You can almost feel yourself getting a headache as you read it, but the second example sets you at ease and causes you to subconsciously relax.    You feel powerful as you notice all the subtle tactics used by the salesperson to remain in a position of power and superiority over the customer.

Now you understand the difference between buying and selling as they relate here.  Please keep this constantly in mind as you read because this is one of the core concepts at the foundation of this system.

# Take Back Your Power

*"Power is the ultimate aphrodisiac."*

*- Henry Kissinger*

Salespeople habitually do things that immediately and unequivocally hand ALL of their power over to prospects and customers, who then hold all the cards and have the sole ability to cause the salesperson to either fail or succeed. Talk about power. The ability to cause someone to succeed or to fail. Think about that for a moment. It's like playing god with someone. That's exactly what it felt like in my early days of selling when prospects wouldn't buy and I had no power to do anything about it, despite the fact that the consequence was being fired from my job.

The worst part about this is the fact that salespeople think they're doing the right thing and that they're SUPPOSED to take these actions that give all their power away. So many times I've heard salespeople say things like:

- "I'm willing to do whatever it takes to earn your business."

- "If you become my customer, I'll be at your beck and call."

- "I'm all about service after the sale. I'll be available to you anytime after installation if you need help."

- "I'll even give you my home number. I want to be available to you anytime for any reason at all."

The salespeople who say these things get themselves into all kinds of bad situations. For starters, entirely too many customers are out to get whatever they can for free and will start acting amazingly sadistic toward salespeople who really are at their beck and call and are willing to do anything at the drop of a hat for the remote possibility that they might get a sale.

A good analogy is to look at people who remain in bad relationships despite the fact that they're hurting themselves by doing so. We can all think of someone, male or female, who chooses to stay in a relationship with someone who is abusive, selfish, or whatever the case may be. They don't leave because they're afraid of being alone or just don't know there's something better out there. This is much like the salesperson who relentlessly cold calls with poor results. Because they've never been taught anything different and have been misled to believe that "cold calling works ... it's a numbers game ... be persistent," they get really desperate and begin selling themselves out to customers in the form of "I'll do anything it takes to earn your business."

In order to gain the respect of anyone, regardless of whether it's in sales situations, personal relationships, etc., you MUST NOT give your power away like that! You must KEEP your power and communicate, very clearly, that YOU are the person who's respect and admiration must be earned.

This concept goes back to what we talked about in the chapter on Why Cold Calling Doesn't Work Anymore. It destroys your status as an equal and makes you appear needy and desperate. You must present yourself as an equal at the very minimum, and preferably as a superior. Then, and only then, will you receive the level of respect from customers necessary to make them fall into a frame of mind that THEY must prove themselves to YOU and EARN a place as your customer.

Please keep in mind that becoming arrogant and brash won't do you any good. Our purpose here is not only to make you recognize that you are an equal as a professional businessperson, but also to make you realize why this frame is an absolute necessity if you are to become hugely successful in the game of selling, which is just that – a game. It's a game of wits and a game of psychological positioning. As for presenting yourself as a superior, well, if you can do that then the game is over before it even begins. Follow this book to the letter and you will be in a position of superiority over your prospects and customers. And, if you happen to come across the occasional egomaniac who gets a sick thrill out of manipulating and humiliating salespeople, you'll have so many leads coming in that you can simply announce, "I'm sorry, I don't have time for this, we can't do business."

Yes, you will be in a position to turn down any prospect who isn't deserving of your time and your consideration. That's the ultimate example of taking back your power. I do it all the time. You have the power. Keep it and use it. Give it to NO ONE.

# It's Not A Numbers Game

*"It's not what you want to sell when you want to sell
it that matters today. It's what the customer wants
to buy when the customer wants to buy it that counts."*

*- John Graham*

It is a well-known fact that a half-truth usually does more harm than a blatant falsehood. The old myth that "sales is a numbers game" is one of these half-truths.

Here's how I see it: If you run into a brick wall once, why on earth would you ever possibly think that running into a brick wall 50 or more times in a day will improve things? In fact, if you keep doing it over and over again, you'll eventually be in a lot worse shape than if you only did it once or not at all.

Unfortunately, this concept is consistently taught to salespeople. Almost all accept it without question, believe it, and adopt it.

How many times have you heard those dreaded words, "You need to increase your activity?" Or perhaps, "The activity isn't there." The universal solution to lagging sales seems to be "more activity." More, more, more.

*IMPORTANT NOTE: The definition of insanity is trying the same thing over and over again with the same end results.*

Here's a novel concept: If your activity isn't getting you the results you want, why do more of the same activity? *Why not change your activity?*

I once had the great misfortune of working for a telecom company that had for a regional director an individual with no sales background whatsoever. His only prior industry experience was working as an engineer for the single most unsuccessful wireless Internet company in the world. On the first business day of every month, this company held an event (concocted, of course, by the unqualified director) called "Beat Your Best." This office was what I like to call a "churn & burn" operation. They had a headcount of about 30 and turned over approximately 30% of the sales force every month. They provided no leads or marketing support and micro-managed the salespeople to do high cold calling activity and to document that activity on daily reports. During "Beat Your Best," every salesperson had to get up in front of the entire branch and display on an overhead projector their previous months' forecast along with their previous months' actual sales. A few salespeople each month would exceed their forecasts. They were supposed to tell a "success story" and, of course, got lots of cheers and applause. Most of the salespeople, as one would expect, fell short of their forecasts. They were required to explain the reasons for this to the group and to announce what they intended to do to fix the mistake and get back on track. Invariably, almost every one of them dropped their head and said things like:

"I didn't do enough activity."

"I need to increase my activity."

"I need to cold call more."

"I'm going to make fifty calls a day."

The managers loved this. They firmly believed that cold calling works, despite the fact that none of them had ever succeeded in sales themselves and got their management positions through connections, relatives, and playing office politics. All of the salespeople agreed as well because they had been taught to cold call, that cold calling works, that sales is a numbers game, and thanks to the micro-managing and daily reports, they were programmed to do it.

All of the salespeople except for one, that is. I sat there every month during this grand spectacle, shaking my head and thinking to myself, "If this person is failing, their activity obviously isn't working. Why would they do more of the same activity? More of the same will equal more failure. The answer is to change the activity from something that clearly isn't working to something that will work."

Naturally, trying to convince anyone else of this was an uphill battle. The management in this particular office was obsessed with cold calling to an extent that was almost cult-like. We had cold call blitzes twice a week, one day on the phones and another day out on the streets, or "canvassing" as they called it. My boss was completely baffled one day when I announced that I no longer desired to participate in the cold call blitzes because I considered them to be a waste of my productive selling time. No matter how hard I tried to explain my reasons or how much logic or how many analogies I used, I couldn't get him to snap out of his years of programming that "cold calling works" and that the solution to any sales slump is to "cold call more" and "increase your activity."

Needless to say, I didn't stay in that position for very much longer. The sad reality is that they are a solid company with a desirable product, but they are shooting themselves in the foot by tying their salespeople's hands behind their backs and saying, "Okay, do it our way. It's our way or the highway." Any company that takes such an attitude would be better off avoiding experienced salespeople and sticking with young, inexperienced rookies right out of school. Not only will they be able to easily mold them in their image, but they'd probably save a ton on salaries as well.

The bottom line is if what you're doing isn't working for you, don't do more of it. Change it. Do something different. Remember, most of the world's successful people got there by working smarter than the rest, not necessarily harder.

# Forget About Persistence

*"Persistence is not profitable. An army is like
a fire. If you do not put it out, it will burn itself out."*

*- Sun Tzu,
The Art Of War*

This idea is closely related to what we discussed in the last chapter, the concept that sales is not a numbers game.

Since I love using true stories from my own personal experiences to relate some of my meanings, here's another one for you to consider. I once had a sales manager who was particularly unsuccessful and subsequently fired. For starters, he ran the office with the old "50-point rule." If you're not familiar with this rule, it states that you start out every day with the requirement of getting 50 points. Every appointment you ran counted for 10 points, and every cold call you made counted for 1 point. So, if you happened to have one appointment scheduled on a particular day, you would be required to make 40 cold calls to make up the balance of your 50 points.

Salespeople who chose to do their cold calls on the phone were required to do them from the office and to fill out a detailed call log, including company name, contact name, telephone number, result of the call, etc. This was so the micro-manager could call 2 or 3 at random to "follow-up," which of course was a way of verifying that the salesperson actually made the calls.

The reps who preferred to do their cold calls in person, which happened to be the majority, were required to be in the office from 5pm to 5:30pm pasting the business cards they picked up to 3x5 index cards and filed away in card boxes. The micro-manager would come around, count everyone's cards to make sure they hit the required number, and initial them to be certain nobody used the same cards twice. (Did I mention that this guy was eventually fired?)

Now here's the kicker, and how this story relates to the title of this chapter: the salespeople were required to keep track of account activity on those 3x5 cards in their card boxes. This manager (remember now, he got fired) firmly believed that every prospect who had received a proposal but not yet bought should be called every single day until they either bought or said no, and so that's what we were all required to do. We had to keep records of this in glorious detail for our random card box inspections, and the end result is that otherwise good prospects were harassed to death and swore never to do business with that company, ever. Persistence at work.

Now let's look at a more down-to-earth example of why I believe that persistence is not profitable, other than the fact that Sun Tzu said so. One of my favorite books of all time on the subject of selling is "How I Raised Myself From Failure To Success In Selling" by Frank Bettger. He points out an astounding fact he realized as the result of keeping detailed records of his activity:

- 70% of his sales were made on the first appointment

- 23% were made on the second appointment

- 7% were made on the third and after

However, *50% of his time was spent chasing that 7% who only bought the third time or after.* By only dealing with customers who bought on the first or second appointment and writing off the ones who did not, he was able to immediately double his income.

The point here is that you must not waste your valuable, productive selling time on anyone who isn't likely to buy. Remember my definitions of buying and selling? If someone is going to buy, they're going to buy. That's that. If you're trying to sell, you're already facing an uphill battle. Isn't it better to take the time you're spending on selling, as I define it, and instead devote that time to the people who want to buy? Do that and you'll probably double your income just like Frank Bettger did in his day. If you do nothing else in this book, do this one thing. It will make the difference.

# Funnels, Forecasts, and other Time Wasters

*"I don't have time for this!"*

*- Typical reaction to a cold call*

What?

Funnels and forecasts are a waste of time?

Well, in theory, no. In reality, yes.

The way I see it, funnels and forecasts are one of those old-school ideas that make sense in theory and look great on paper but backfire in practice.

How many times have you heard trainers and managers talk about the importance of proper "funnel management?" I heard it entirely too many times and it made me sick to my stomach.

For starters, if you happen to be a sales manager and you're reading this, immediately stop using the word "funnel" with your salespeople. In fact, eliminate the word from your vocabulary entirely unless you happen to need one to add transmission fluid to your car (in my opinion, the only appropriate use of the word funnel).

Sales managers talk about funnels and funnel reviews and funnel management without considering a basic principle of psychology. The word "funnel" has entirely too many negative connotations attached to it. For most salespeople, "funnel review" is synonymous with micro-management, probation, and "performance improvement plans." In other words, just hearing the word "funnel" is usually enough to instantly change a salesperson's frame from positive to negative. This happens subconsciously and the salesperson isn't consciously aware of it, other than the fact that for some reason their level of enthusiasm drops significantly and they don't know why. Review the chapter on Overcoming Limiting Beliefs for more on how this mechanism of the mind works.

(If you're one of those "little dictator" sales managers who is aware of this and throws the terms "funnel" and "funnel review" around in a blatant attempt to terrorize your salespeople and "keep them on their toes," do me a favor and immediately discard this book and contact my company for a refund. You have no place in the professional world of selling and I want to have nothing to do with you. I consider it a disparagement to my reputation to even have this book sitting on your bookshelf.)

There are a few, more practical reasons why I disagree with the use of funnels and forecasts, at least in the ways they're typically used. Let me give you an example. I once had a sales manager who was obsessive with "funnel management" and always lectured us about how it's the key to success in selling and that without proper funnel management, there was no hope for success or even survival. He insisted that any salesperson must have at least 500% of their quota in the "proposal" stage of their funnel at all times, no matter what.

I had a problem agreeing with this for several reasons but one stood out in particular. I learned early on that in the telecom industry, the average closing ratio was 20-25% and a really good salesperson would close about 30%. That's the logic behind proposing 500% every month.

The upper management at Lucent would obsess over different minute details at different times, and for a while it was closing ratios. For a while we had a board up on a wall in the office listing everyone's closing ratios, in descending order, every month. I had the usual 25% closing ratio in my early days, at least until that day one of my mentors taught me the secret to sales success: "Instead of contacting random people who will NEVER buy your product, create and enact systems to uncover the people who WANT to buy your product." After a few months of taking that advice and putting it to work, I was sitting at the top of the list with an 80% closing ratio, absolutely unheard of in that industry.

The reason why I cannot agree with the idea of proposing 500% of quota every month in order to make 100% of quota is because any salesperson who does so is obviously achieving only a lowly 20% closing ratio. Instead of addressing the REAL problem of a low close rate, which almost always has behind it a failure to properly qualify prospects up-front, proposing 500% of quota is merely another way of saying "increase your activity" and we've already established the fact that "increasing your activity" is not the solution to all of life's problems, as many sales managers would have us believe.

The title of this chapter uses the term "Time Wasters" to refer to funnels but "Success Destroyer" would probably be more accurate. As you can see, dwelling on funnel management results only in generating more and more activity without correcting the core problems. It's like taking aspirin to cure chronic headaches instead of eliminating the underlying causes such as stress or poor nutrition. You're only kidding yourself by doing so.

Dwelling and obsessing over funnel management and using it as a tool to plan and conduct sales activities does nothing more than hide the real problems behind a salesperson's lack of success and exhaust the salesperson with high levels of unpleasant, fruitless activity. The solution instead should be as follows:

- Do a better job of finding and attracting good, qualified prospects

- Do a better job of qualifying prospects out instead of presenting a proposal to anyone who shows mild interest just for the sake of listing them on your funnel and satisfying the imaginary need for "high activity"

- Do a better job of developing proper solutions for prospects

- Do a better job of presenting, overcoming objections, and closing (something that shouldn't be an issue if the salesperson thoroughly qualified the prospect at the beginning)

Now let's shift our discussion to forecasts.

Forecasts are necessary, to some extent, in the operation of a business. Any successful business obviously has proper planning behind it and semi-accurate forecasting is necessary to accomplish this.

The problems begin when forecasting is misused by the salespeople, the management, or both.

We all know how salespeople misuse forecasts. The vast majority of salespeople are overly optimistic on forecasts because they want to make the boss happy and at least appear to be on track to hit their numbers. Salespeople routinely leave deals they already know they've lost on their forecasts. Personally, I always underestimated forecasts or left deals off entirely because there's nothing I hate more than some manager who has entirely too much time on his hands breathing down my neck, asking me on a daily basis, "When is this one going to sign? When is that one going to sign?" Either way, the end result is that the forecast is inaccurate and therefore the entire purpose of having them is defeated.

Management misuses forecasts in a variety of ways, from the silly to the downright stupid. Remember the sales manager I mentioned who was obsessed with the idea of funnel management? Well, his boss was obsessed with accurate forecasting and took it to such an extreme that it destroyed morale, made people quit, and caused sales to suffer dearly in the end.

This guy implemented a requirement that all salespeople and sales managers within his organization absolutely must forecast to within 10% accuracy each and every week. He called the forecasted number the "commitment" and nobody was allowed to deviate more than 10% from their commitment. He even went so far as to create elaborate spreadsheets that generated detailed reports as to who was meeting their commitments, who was off-track, if so by how much, and was complete with lots of pretty graphs and pie charts. By the way, you got in trouble for exceeding your commitment by more than 10% just as much as if you fell short by more than 10%. If that isn't lunacy, I don't know what is.

(Interestingly, when I pressed him to explain to me why this must be so, he admitted that he had absolutely nothing to do one day and so he spent – or should I say WASTED - several hours concocting this idiotic plan. He is a grand example of someone who contributes nothing to an organization and should be immediately fired or have his position eliminated.)

The reality of the situation boils down to another one of those basic facts of the selling profession that is so often overlooked:

**As salespeople, we cannot control sales. We can only control our sales activities.**

In other words, once we've properly gone through all the steps of a sale and "asked for the order," it's out of our hands. There can be a variety of reasons why someone who should buy can't or won't. They're too numerous to mention here. Just when I think I've seen and heard them all, another more absurd one comes along. I've had situations where I had already secured a verbal commitment and it was a sure thing, and I never found out why they didn't buy and never heard from them again. I've had customers sign contracts, then decide to withhold payment and cancel the order. These things happen. Attempting to hold salespeople accountable is irresponsible and unrealistic, and is the act of an upper management that has never been in real-life selling situations. These people leave school with their MBAs, are hired directly into management, and spend the rest of their lives sitting comfortably behind desks, buried in spreadsheets, looking at cute pie charts and graphs. Granted, there are plenty of salespeople out there who are downright lazy, out to collect a salary for as long as they possibly can, and will never make their forecasts or hit their numbers. They should be fired and eventually will be. For the rest of us, who are out to make an honest living and work hard every day, we can only do our best to work smart and hard, improve ourselves in as many ways as possible, and never stop the learning process.

# Filters and Amplifiers

*"...after I gave my pitch, Mr. Edison got up, walked all around me, looked me over, smiled, and said 'Now what is it you came to see me about, young man?' That's how I found out Mr. Edison was hard of hearing. Now I had to explain myself all over again, loudly. I had a three days' growth of beard, my shoes were scuffed, and my clothes looked dusty and shabby."*

*- Edwin Barnes,*
*the only business partner Thomas A. Edison ever had,*
*describing his very first meeting with Mr. Edison*

The world of marketing has a term called "filters and amplifiers." Because what we intend to teach you in this program is your own mini-marketing program, it is necessary for you to understand some of the basics of marketing and this one is perhaps the most important.

Put simply, a filter is something that impedes you and an amplifier is something that helps you. In other words, an amplifier assists in helping to get your message across and a filter blocks your message.

Marketing people take this concept of filters and amplifiers to minute detail that seems almost ridiculous. For example, direct mail marketers use the concept to determine which way a sales letter will be folded and inserted into an envelope. If the letter is folded with the type in the inside, that's considered a filter because you have to take the extra step of removing and unfolding the letter before you can start reading the sales message. On the other hand, if the letter is folded in such a manner that the type is immediately visible upon opening the envelope, it's considered an amplifier because it's getting your message to the prospective customer more quickly.

Keep this concept in mind. Evaluate each and every action you take as to whether it's a filter or an amplifier. Go to the ridiculous, minute detail that the direct marketers do. Remember, filters are bad. Amplifiers are good.

# You Are What You Wear:
# The Powerful Effects of Image

*"Everything is judged by its appearance; what is unseen counts for nothing. Never let yourself get lost in the crowd, then, or buried in oblivion. Stand out. Be conspicuous, at all cost. Make yourself a magnet of attention by appearing larger, more colorful, more mysterious than the bland and timid masses."*

*Robert Greene and Joost Elffers*
*"The 48 Laws of Power"*

I am a firm believer in the power of image and the idea that perception is everything. Anyone who has worked with me in sales knows that I take this concept to extremes and attain tremendous results with it.

There is another dangerous half-truth running around out there in our world of selling that I believe is literally destroying the careers of otherwise very talented salespeople. It is the misconception that "you should dress like your prospects." This is based on the belief that dressing like your prospects will build instant rapport, put them at ease, and therefore increase your chances of getting the sale.

If you've already read the chapters Buying vs. Selling and Take Back Your Power, you know that putting prospects at ease and making them feel comfortable around me is the absolute LAST thing I want to do. It's like shooting yourself in the foot with a very large gun. Remember those examples of salespeople who give away their power and endure the wrath of sadistic, selfish prospects and customers? This is another sure-fire way to wind up in that situation.

I do not believe that you should dress like your prospects. I firmly believe that you should DRESS LIKE THE PEOPLE THEY TURN TO FOR ADVICE.

Who are the people in our society who are turned to for advice? Attorneys, accountants, management consultants, financial advisors, marketing consultants, etc. Think of how these people typically dress and present themselves.

Why do most people take the advice of doctors without question, when that advice frequently is to undergo expensive, painful, and sometimes dangerous surgery? Because of the powerful *image* associated with doctors. Their authority is not questioned. Believe it or not, the medical industry knows and uses things about image and positioning that most people in our industry just don't know. Do your prospects respect you as much as they respect their doctors? If not, why not? Do something to change that.

Why is the stereotypical image of a lawyer associated with a dark, expensive suit, a red power tie, and slicked-back hair? Because, much like doctors, lawyers and the legal industry work hard to maintain and project an image of power and intimidation. Why don't you?

The fact that it's much easier to say "no" to someone you're comfortable with than it is to someone who intimidates you is a proven fact of psychology. Think of the world of relationships and dating. Early in a relationship, the two lovebirds are doing all the usual dating and courtship behaviors such as going out to nice elegant dinners together. They're eager to please each other and if one person asks for a favor, the other is more than happy to do it. Why? Because they're not overly comfortable with each other yet. Each of the lovebirds feels slightly intimidated by the other, and as a result it's hard to say "no" to anything the other person may request.

What happens after a year? Are the two lovebirds still spending their time together gazing into each other's eyes over a candlelight table? No! They're doing plain old normal things that people do on a daily basis, such as shopping, cooking dinner at home, watching television, etc. And are they still ready, willing, and eager to say "yes" anytime the other person asks a favor? Probably not! They're now deep in the comfort zone. The need for approval is gone and the fear of loss is gone.

The same applies in selling situations. It's best to carry yourself with an air of superiority and an aura of prosperity. Not only does it communicate that you don't need the prospect's business, it also communicates that you don't need their approval on any level.

Here's a comparison to demonstrate what I'm talking about. I'll use myself compared to most of the competition I've seen out there:

The typical competing salesperson I've seen will arrive for the appointment wearing a polo or golf shirt, khakis, and casual shoes, usually with a cell phone or pager clipped to the belt. They're carrying some type of planner or binder and a Bic pen, perhaps along with product brochures to give the prospect. They're trying to be overly cheery and smiley and come off as sort of goofy and everyone instantly knows there's a salesman in the house. Chances are the cell phone is turned on and may even ring loudly while the salesperson is waiting for the prospect. Finally, the prospect comes out, welcomes the salesperson, and leads him back to the prospect's office. The salesperson, upon entering, will look around and attempt to start a conversation based on something in the office. This is the old sales training "talk about something in the office in an attempt to build rapport" scheme. Or perhaps there will be some conversation about where the prospect is originally from, where in town they live, etc. (I used to do this myself and it just annoys prospects. They know you're there to try and sell something and it's better to cut to the chase.) The salesperson then goes into the company story routine, which sends a subconscious message to the prospect that the salesperson is in need of approval and is telling the story despite the fact that the prospect never asked. Perhaps there's a flipchart or power point presentation to go along with it. The remainder of the appointment goes as usual, with the typical fact-finding, questioning, and other necessary elements to the sales process.

Here's how I like to go about conducting an appointment. I arrive dressed to the nines, wearing a nice suit, always with the jacket on despite how hot it may be outside, and with everything in perfect order. A cell phone is nowhere in sight – in fact, it's sitting in my car, turned off. I'm carrying a nice leather-bound journal with gold edge pages along with a Montblanc fountain pen, the same one I will use to write with during the appointment. I announce that I'm there to see so-and-so and take a seat. No "salesman" alarm sirens go off and the receptionist wonders if the company is being sued or bought out. When the prospect comes out, I introduce myself in a very conservative, composed manner and don't act overly excited to be there, or "salesy" as I like to put it. I follow the prospect into his office, unbutton my suit jacket, and sit down only after the prospect either sits first or says "have a seat." Although I may notice some interesting things in the office, I don't comment on any of them and make no attempt whatsoever to build rapport. He and I both know why I'm there and I get right down to business. Remember how I said a sure way to offend a busy executive is to waste his or her time? Don't do it, especially now that you're face-to-face with a live prospect. The remainder of the appointment goes as usual, I thank the prospect, and leave quietly. I avoid the company story routine unless the prospect asks specific questions about my company, which I of course answer as accurately as possible. (Why do I not tell a company story? Because all the research and surveys done on the subject prove that prospects really don't care to hear it and consider it a waste of time. It works as a filter against you.)

What happened there? Why is my way of presenting myself and doing things different? Because an aura of confidence, and to a lesser degree, and aura of mystery is given off. If I was neck-and-neck with one or more of my competitors, that just changed. The prospect is thinking, "Wow, that guy was different. He looked and acted a lot more professional than the others and made no attempt to kiss up to me or build phony rapport like all the other typical salesmen did. He must really have his act together and know his stuff."

Nowadays, the concepts of business causal and "dress like your prospect" are rampant. The problem is that most people don't understand just why it's so important to dress well. With that in mind, here's an excerpt from my favorite book, "The Law Of Success," written by my all-time favorite author, Napoleon Hill, which I've included now that the book is in the public domain. As you read, keep in mind that this was written in the 1920s and to multiply the prices mentioned by at least ten. Also remember that the story may be old but human psychology never changes:

## The Psychology Of Good Clothes

When the good news came from the theater of war, on November the eleventh, 1918, my worldly possessions amounted to but little more than they did the day I came into the world.

The war had destroyed my business and made it necessary for me to make a new start!

My wardrobe consisted of three well worn business suits and two uniforms which I no longer needed.

Knowing all too well that the world forms its first and most lasting impressions of a man by the clothes he wears, I lost no time in visiting my tailor.

Happily, my tailor had known me for many years, therefore he did not judge me entirely by the clothes I wore. If he had I would have been "sunk."

With less than a dollar in change in my pocket, I picked out the cloth for three of the most expensive suits I ever owned, and ordered that they be made up for me at once.

The three suits came to $375.00!

I shall never forget the remark made by the tailor as he took my measure. Glancing first at the three bolts of expensive cloth which I had selected, and then at me, he inquired:

"Dollar-a-year man, eh?"

"No," said I, "if I had been fortunate enough to get on the dollar-a-year payroll I might now have enough money to pay for these suits."

The tailor looked at me with surprise. I don't think he got the joke.

One of the suits was a beautiful dark gray; one was a dark blue; the other was a light blue with a pin stripe.

Fortunately, I was in good standing with my tailor, therefore he did not ask when I was going to pay for those expensive suits.

I knew that I could and would pay for them in due time, but could I have convinced him of that? This was the thought which was running through my mind, with hope against hope that the question would not be brought up.

I then visited my haberdasher, from whom I purchased three less expensive suits and a complete supply of the best shirts, collars, ties, hosiery and underwear that he carried.

My bill at the haberdasher's amounted to a little over $300.00.

With an air of prosperity I nonchalantly signed the charge ticket and tossed it back to the salesman, with instructions to deliver my purchase the following morning.   The feeling of renewed self-reliance and success had begun to come over me, even before I had attired myself in my newly purchased outfit.

I was out of the war and $675.00 in debt, all in less than twenty-four hours.

The following day the first of the three suits ordered from the haberdasher was delivered.  I put it on at once, stuffed a new silk handkerchief in the outside pocket of my coat, shoved the $50.00 I had borrowed on my ring down into my pants pocket, and walked down Michigan Boulevard, in Chicago, feeling as rich as Rockefeller.

Every article of clothing I wore, from my underwear out, was of the very best.  That it was not paid for was nobody's business except mine and my tailor's and my haberdasher's.

Every morning I dressed myself in an entirely new outfit, and walked down the same street, at precisely the same hour.  That hour "happened" to be the time when a certain wealthy publisher usually walked down the same street, on his way to lunch.

I made it my business to speak to him each day, and occasionally I would stop for a minute's chat with him.

After this daily meeting had been going on for about a week I met this publisher one day, but decided I would see if he would let me get by without speaking.

Watching him from under my eyelashes I looked straight ahead, and started to pass him when he stopped and motioned me over to the edge of the sidewalk, placed his hand on my shoulder, and said:  "You look damned prosperous for a man who has just laid aside a uniform.  Who makes your clothes?"

"Well," said I, "Wilkie & Sellery made this particular suit."

He then wanted to know what sort of business I was engaged in.  That "airy" atmosphere of prosperity which I had been wearing, along with a new and different suit every day, had got the better of his curiosity.  (I had hoped that it would.)

Flipping the ashes from my Havana perfecto, I said "Oh, I am preparing the copy for a new magazine that I am going to publish."

"A new magazine, eh?" he queried, "and what are you going to call it?"

"It is to be named Hill's Golden Rule."

"Don't forget," said my publisher friend, "that I am in the business of printing and distributing magazines.  Perhaps I can serve you, also."

That was the moment for which I had been waiting. I had that very moment, and almost the very spot of ground on which we stood, in mind when I was purchasing those new suits.

But, is it necessary to remind you, that conversation never would have taken place had this publisher observed me walking down that street from day to day, with a "whipped-dog" look on my face, an un-pressed suit on my back and a look of poverty in my eyes.

An appearance of prosperity attracts attention always, with no exceptions whatsoever. Moreover, a look of prosperity attracts "favorable attention," because the one dominating desire in every human heart is to be prosperous.

My publisher friend invited me to his club for lunch. Before the coffee and cigars had been served he had "talked me out of" the contract for printing and distributing my magazine. I had even "consented" to permit him to supply the capital, without any interest charge.

For the benefit of those who are not familiar with the publishing business may I not offer the information that considerable capital is required for launching a new nationally distributed magazine.

Capital, in such large amounts, is often hard to get, even with the best of security. The capital necessary for launching Hill's Golden Rule magazine, which you may have read, was well above $30,000.00, and every cent of it was raised on a "front" created mostly by good clothes. True, there may have been some ability back of those clothes, but many millions of men have ability who never have anything else, and who are never heard of outside of the limited community in which they live. This is a rather sad truth!

To some it may seem an unpardonable extravagance for one who was "broke" to have gone in debt for $675.00 worth of clothes, but the psychology back of that investment more than justified it.

The appearance of prosperity not only made a favorable impression on those to whom I had to look for favors, but of more importance still was the effect that proper attire HAD ON ME.

I not only knew that correct clothes would impress others favorably, but I knew that good clothes would give me an atmosphere of self-reliance, without which I could not hope to regain my lost fortunes.

I got my first training in the psychology of good clothes from my friend Edwin C. Barnes, who is a close business associate of Thomas A. Edison. Barnes afforded considerable amusement for the Edison staff when he rode into West Orange on a freight train (not being able to raise sufficient money for the passenger fare) and announced at the Edison offices that he had come to enter into a partnership with Mr. Edison.

Nearly everyone around the Edison plant laughed at Barnes, except Edison himself. He saw something in the square jaw and determined face of young Barnes which most of the others did not see, despite the fact that the young man looked more like a tramp than he did a future partner of the greatest inventor on earth.

Barnes got his start, sweeping floors in the Edison offices!

That was all he sought – just a chance to get a toe-hold in the Edison organization. From there on he made history that is well worth emulation by other young men who wish to make places for themselves.

Barnes has now retired from active business, even though he is still a comparatively young man, and spends most of his time at his two beautiful homes in Bradentown, Florida, and Damariscotta, Maine. He is a multimillionaire, prosperous and happy.

I first became acquainted with Barnes during the early days of his association with Edison, before he had "arrived."

In those days he had the largest and most expensive collection of clothes I had ever seen or heard of one man owning. His wardrobe consisted of thirty-one suits; one for each day of the month. He never wore the same suit two days in succession.

Moreover, all his suits were of the most expensive type. (Incidentally, his clothes were made by the same tailors who made those three suits for me.)

He wore socks which cost six dollars per pair.

His shirts and other wearing apparel cost in similar proportion. His cravats were specially made, at a cost of from five to seven dollars and a half each.

One day, in a spirit of fun, I asked him to save some of his old suits which he did not need, for me.

He informed me that he hadn't a single suit which he did not need!

He then gave me a lesson on the psychology of good clothes which is well worth remembering. "I do not wear thirty-one suits of clothes," said he, "entirely for the impression they make on other people; I do it mostly for the impression they have on me."

Barnes then told me of the day when he presented himself at the Edison plant, for a position. He said he had to walk around the plant a dozen times before he worked up enough courage to announce himself, because he knew that he looked more like a tramp than he did a desirable employee.

Barnes is said to be the most able salesman ever connected with the great inventor of West Orange. His entire fortune was made through his ability as a salesman, but he has often said that he never could have accomplished the results which have made him both wealthy and famous had it not been for his understanding of the psychology of good clothes.

I have met many salesmen in my time. During the past ten years I have personally trained and directed the efforts of more than 3,000 salespeople, both men and women, and I have observed that, without a single exception, the star producers were all people who understood and made good use of the psychology of clothes.

I have seen a few well dressed people who made no outstanding records as salesmen, but I have yet to see the first poorly dressed man who became a star producer in the field of selling.

I have studied the psychology of clothes for so long, and I have watched its effect on people in so many different walks of life, that I am fully convinced there is a close connection between clothes and success.

Take that story to heart as you power up your image and apply the psychology of good clothes to your own life. I have. The results will truly astound you.

# Overcoming Limiting Beliefs

*"If I've said it once, I've said it a thousand times. I consider cold calling a waste of time."*

*- Jeffrey Gitomer*

You guessed it – more psychology!

The reason for spending time on some of the psychological background of successful selling is because I firmly believe that in order for the techniques to really work for you, or your "outer game" as I call it, you must first get your "inner game" in order, and most importantly, you must get rid of the limiting beliefs you have in your mind that are probably holding you back from achieving great success.

Your subconscious mind is always at work. Day and night, while you're awake and especially while you sleep, your subconscious is always thinking and processing information. The problem has to do with the fact that it cannot differentiate between positive and negative – it merely works with the information handed over to it from the conscious mind – and because it never stops working, if it has nothing other than negative thoughts to work with, it will.

Information and thoughts can only be handed over from the conscious mind to the subconscious if they are continuously repeated in the conscious mind and emotionally charged. The term self-suggestion or autosuggestion is the process of repeating a thought to oneself, over and over again in a state of emotion, until it finally reaches the subconscious and is acted upon.

The effectiveness of this process has been known for over a century and has been proven in various studies. For example, smokers who had repeatedly tried to quit and failed were given statements and were instructed to say these statements several times out loud in front of a mirror immediately upon arising, once during the course of the day, and, most importantly, immediately before going to bed at night. They were to say these statements as emotionally as possible and to really feel the power and emotion behind the message as strongly as possible. The statements went something like this:

"Smoking is a filthy, disgusting habit. Only the most worthless, low-down people smoke. I don't do it because I hate it, it disgusts me, and it makes me physically sick. I can't stand the smell and the taste is downright repulsive. Just the thought of a cigarette makes me nauseous to the point that I want to vomit. I hate smoking."

The subjects who followed the instructions to the letter and repeated the statement to themselves with strong emotion were unable to even pick up a cigarette after a few weeks of this. These are people who had been trying to quit, unsuccessfully, for years.

Most people inadvertently cause this same principle to work against themselves, and usually manage do it while they're trying to help or improve themselves in one way or another. This is because of a lack of common knowledge about the internal workings of the human mind. It was the belief of Andrew Carnegie, Thomas Edison, and many other successful people that these principles should be taught in school and, if they were, would cut the average time needed to complete school in half.

Here's an example of how salespeople cause this principle to backfire and actually cause more harm than good. The problem lies in the fact that salespeople give themselves directives that cause the subconscious to dwell upon and therefore amplify the negative. Let's consider some things an up-and-coming salesperson might ask him or herself in an attempt to improve:

- "How can I overcome my fear of rejection?"

  Although salespeople who ask this question of themselves don't realize it, it causes the mind to focus on FEAR and REJECTION rather than positive virtues. Keep in mind that any thoughts that reach the subconscious mind are accepted by it, processed, and the end result is fed back to the conscious mind for the purpose of being put into action.

  Asking oneself how to get over fear and rejection causes the subconscious to recognize the key points of FEAR and REJECTION, then feed back to the conscious mind ways and means of feeling even more FEAR and REJECTION, thereby paralyzing the salesperson's mind with these emotions and destroying any chances for success.

- "How can I overcome frustration in day-to-day selling?"

  Once again, this is a question that focuses on a negative virtue, in this case FRUSTRATION. After a salesperson spends enough time thinking about it and asking the question of him or herself, the idea of FRUSTRATION will eventually reach the subconscious mind through the principle of autosuggestion. The subconscious will act on it and send back to the conscious mind an even stronger feeling and fear of FRUSTRATION.

- "How can I avoid feeling stupid or doing dumb things in sales situations?"

  Here, the salesperson is inadvertently using the principle of autosuggestion to feed the ideas of feeling stupid and doing dumb things to the subconscious. Guess what? The subconscious acts upon it and gives the conscious mind instructions on how to do even more dumb things and how to feel even stupider, and that's exactly what happens.

Your subconscious mind is like a fertile garden spot that always manages to fill up with weeds. Anyone who keeps a garden or takes pride in having a beautiful yard knows there are always a few fertile spots where no matter what you do, weeds just seem to keep popping up. That's because fertile soil is fertile to any kind of seeds that happen to land there, no matter what they are. It cannot differentiate between good and bad seeds. That's exactly how your subconscious operates. It takes whatever is fed to it and works with it, good or bad. It's your responsibility to make sure that only good, positive thoughts reach your subconscious mind and to keep the bad, negative thoughts out.

How to do this? One of the simplest and most effective ways is to be on guard for negative thoughts, questions, and self-doubts, and to re-frame them in a positive light. Re-framing is the process of taking a negative perspective and asking the same question from a positive point of view. Let's use the aforementioned examples to demonstrate this:

- "How can I overcome my fear of rejection?" might become "I'm happy to hear 'no' because it means I'm closer to 'yes'" or, even better, "Who cares what happens? In every situation I'm indifferent to the outcome."

- "How can I overcome frustration in day-to-day selling?" might become "How can I be happy and in a good mood during my day-to-day selling?" or, even better, "I feel healthy, I feel happy, I feel terrific, and nothing bothers me, ever."

- "How can I avoid feeling stupid or doing dumb things in sales situations?" becomes "I'm the best at what I do and am an expert. I inspire awe and respect from the people I do business with." Or, you might even say to yourself "I don't care what anyone thinks regardless of what the outcome is, because it doesn't matter anyway."

Write a positive statement about yourself. It can be as simple as the "I feel healthy, I feel happy, I feel terrific!" used by W. Clement Stone. Repeat your positive self-image statement to yourself throughout the day, but most importantly right before you go to sleep at night, preferably as you lay in bed.

*It is especially important to feed positive thoughts and images to your subconscious mind right before you go to sleep because your subconscious works hardest while you sleep. The thoughts you think before falling asleep will determine, to a large degree, how you feel when you wake up in the morning and how your entire day will be. When you have a bad day, it's almost certainly because you thought about problems or worries before going to sleep the night before. Think positive at bedtime at all costs!*

This principle of carefully directing your thoughts before going to bed at night is also the reason many motivational speakers and coaches recommend reviewing your to-do list and your next day's activities right before going to bed. It allows that information to be processed by your subconscious mind as you sleep, and in many cases you'll wake up with fresh, new ideas that will contribute to your tasks that day. When you have seemingly brilliant ideas that seem to flash into your mind from out of "thin air," that's your subconscious mind talking to you.

Interestingly, Thomas A. Edison had the solution for the incandescent electric lamp handed over to him by his subconscious mind in a dream as he napped one day. Mr. Edison slept only three to four hours every night and took several fifteen-minute naps during the day to make up the deficit. The problem at the time was that he could get a wire to glow as an electric current passed through it, but the wire would burn out very quickly. During one long, particularly frustrating day in which Mr. Edison failed at several attempts to build a light bulb and prevent the wire from burning out, he drifted off to sleep. As Mr. Edison fell asleep, he had a vivid dream of a piece of wood burning brightly and quickly reducing down to ashes. His dream then shifted to a piece of charcoal underneath the ashes continuing to glow for a long time. As he awoke, he realized that the wood quickly burned down to ashes because it was exposed to oxygen but the charcoal burned brightly for hours because it was choked off from the air. He immediately took a piece of wire, put it inside a jar, pumped out all the air, hooked it up to an electric current, and at that very moment the world's first incandescent electric lamp was born, a product of the creative vision of Mr. Edison's subconscious mind which was hard at work on the problem as he slept.

# The Amazing Power of Leverage

Salespeople tend to limit themselves by not using the power of leverage.

In order to understand the power of leverage, imagine a 200-pound boulder that you need to move out of the way. You push up against it, shoulder it, throw all your weight against it, and if you happen to be big and strong enough, it might give just a little.

Now image you have a long plank – a lever – that you can stick underneath the boulder. You push down on the other end and the boulder rolls over with ease.

Now, with that image in mind, think of a salesperson who has a steep quota, no company-provided leads, no referrals, and is out beating the streets walking into one door at a time, or is pounding the phone trying to find prospects. It's a race against the clock. Time is running out, that quota isn't getting any smaller, and the salesperson is losing the race. It's like trying to move that massive boulder all by yourself.

Shift now to the image of a salesperson who doesn't need to "hit the streets" or "dial for dollars" because of a few simple systems that are at work in the background. Prospects are being contacted in a variety of ways with the salesperson's pitch and contact information. Perhaps some are searching the Internet for the salesperson's product and happen to come upon that salesperson's website. It's like having three or four salespeople doing the job of prospecting. Although that salesperson can only be in one place at one time physically, he or she has found virtual ways to be in many places at once, all actively prospecting for new business.

The difference is clear – one is working smart and the other is working hard. It's also clear that the hard-working salesperson is probably putting in twice as many hours and getting half the results as the smart-working salesperson.

Another of my favorite authors, Robert T. Kiyosaki, author of the "Rich Dad, Poor Dad" series of books and tapes talks about the power of leverage in becoming a business owner as opposed to being an employee or self-employed person. The same principle can be applied here. An overly simplified explanation of what he talks about is that an employee or self-employed individual (such as a doctor or lawyer) must work in order to have income. If the person stops working, the income stops as well. A business owner, on the other hand, owns a system of generating income that continues to work whether the owner chooses to or not.

Your goal must be to create and own a mini-marketing system that will continue to generate leads for you on a regular and consistent basis whether you choose to work that particular day or not. As with a business system, there's work involved in building your marketing system, but once it's up and running it will take care of itself and give you a steady supply of leads.

The real value of this program and the only way to benefit from it in a big way is to keep the concept of systems and leverage in mind at all times, and to develop your own personalized program around it. You may have used one or more of the techniques in this book with some degree of success, but the key is to use as many of the techniques as possible *as consistently as possible.* Then, and only then, will you have more leads than you can handle and will you be able to forever eliminate the horrors of cold calling from your life.

# How to Succeed In Sales

*"I'm gonna make you rich....*
*This is your wake-up call, pal.*
*Go to work."*

*- Gordon Gekko to Bud Fox,*
*in "Wall Street"*

Now it's time to move on to the actual methods, techniques, and strategies that I like to call Information Age sales techniques. I refer to them as Information Age because the entire purpose is to disseminate your information or your message to as many prospects as possible as quickly and consistently as possible.

Before you can disseminate your message, you have to create it. This chapter will cover the basic guidelines as to what your message should be. I cannot create your message for you. You and only you can do that. A lot of factors come into play, including your product, your personality and style of selling, your company, your market, your price, and on and on. However, there are a number of mistakes commonly made by salespeople who attempt to create a marketing & prospecting system for themselves without understanding some basics of marketing.

The basic guidelines and mistakes to avoid are as follows:

## Use bait

Announcing to the world that you sell a product or service that hundreds of other salespeople happen to sell probably won't get you a good response. Do something to entice the prospect, get their attention, or communicate that you can provide something nobody else can. For example, I recently read about an insurance agency that once offered to buy small contractors "the biggest steak dinner in town" if the firm couldn't save them money on their business insurance. Guess what? Their phone rang. The competition's didn't.

I was able to excel in telecom sales by finding the real needs of prospects and telling them I could fulfill them. All the other sales reps were going with the message of "we can save you money on your local and long-distance phone bills" and failing miserably because nobody cared. In fact, they were sick and tired of hearing it from ten other salespeople every week. I went with "high-speed Internet available everywhere!" and my phone rang off the hook. I got the business. They didn't.

## Target the right people

Don't communicate your message to people who can't act upon it. Addressing mail to "owner" or "office manager" won't cut it. Spending time with a general manager in a company where the owner makes all the decisions and ignores the manager's opinion altogether is a waste of your time and theirs.

## Be creative

This goes back to the first point.  While all the other insurance agencies in town said "we can save you money," the one who said "we'll buy you dinner if we can't save you money" got the business.  While all the other salespeople were saying "we can save you money on your bills," I claimed "Internet access everywhere!" and I got the calls, even the ones where I couldn't get them Internet but got their local and long-distance service anyway.

## Focus on what prospects really want

Again, this is redundant, but why push what you're selling instead of giving them what they want?  Remember the difference between buying and selling?  Apply that concept to your product.  Re-frame your mind away from a selling frame and into a buying frame.  Ask the all-important question, "what will make a prospect pick up the phone and BUY from me?"

My marketing materials in the telecom days contained something interesting.  Telecom salesmen are right up there with used car salesman for having a reputation for being decidedly obnoxious and unprofessional.  To overcome that and entice prospects to call me, my flyers and mailers contained the following line:

"Don't deal with pushy telecom salespeople!  Call today!"

The obvious irony is that I was a telecom salesperson, but I found a creative way to give the prospects what they wanted – a way to buy the services they needed without "having to deal with pushy telecom salesmen."  This is good proof of the power of image and positioning.  *You can make yourself whoever you want to be in the prospect's eyes.*

## Don't let them form an opinion of you – do it for them

If you don't tell people up front why you and your company are the best and why they should do business with you, they won't.  I've said it before and I'll say it again – perception is everything.  To take it a step further, in sales, perception is *reality*.  Differentiate yourself and your company in creative ways.  Look at Avis and their "We Try Harder" slogan.  It worked.

## Offer them something outstanding

It could be free installation, free this-or-that, an unconditional money-back guarantee, or something else that's too good to turn down.  The Godfather made "an offer he couldn't refuse" and author Mark Joyner talks about making an Irresistible Offer. What's yours?

## Be in the right place at the right time

How many times have you heard a prospect say, "Oh, we just bought one of those a few weeks ago, too bad you didn't call us sooner, maybe we would have bought from you."

Timing is essential. You need to be in the right place at the right time, right?

True, but let's take it a step further. To succeed in the Information Age, you need to be *in all places at all times*. You need to come at your prospects from many different angles and in a variety of ways. Keep your message in front of them at all times. Then, and only then, will you be in all places at all times and avoid the unpleasantness of "oh, you're just a little bit too late."

## Name yourself or your product

Don't be "Your territory account manager" or "your local representative." Be "Your certified expert on *<your product>*, offering free unbiased recommendations based on your needs."

Be larger than life. Remember, perception is reality to your prospects and you can be whoever or whatever you want to be. Be conspicuous at all costs. What is unseen counts for nothing. It's entirely up to you.

## Be consistent and never slow down

Persistence isn't profitable in selling, but it's everything in running a marketing system. Momentum will build as a result of consistent effort. Create a schedule for the various elements of your system and stick with it no matter what.

## Get rid of the company story B.S.

Remember those studies I mentioned proving that prospects couldn't care less about your company story? Keep it off your marketing materials as well. Nobody is interested in knowing that you're a public company, how long you've been in business, who your CEO is, or anything else for that matter. In fact, in some cases I've gotten better results by not even including a company name at all. You won't miss out on calls from prospects who may have had a bad experience with your company in the past and you will present yourself as more of a consultant, something we'll talk about later.

## Get your prospects into action now

Create a sense of urgency. Make them think they've got something to lose by not contacting you immediately. One easy way to do this is to include a "limited-time offer," most likely associated with your hook. If you're going to advertise free installation, no setup costs, waived application fees or whatever your hook is, make it for a limited time. Give them a reason to call you NOW instead of filing your materials away with the other ones they received and never acted upon.

## Make it easy for them to respond

Your materials *must* include several different ways to contact you. Include an office number, a cell number, an email address, and especially a fax-back form. Fax-back forms generate a tremendous response you'd otherwise miss out on and almost nobody is using them.

A fax-back form is merely a few fill-in-the-blank lines at the bottom of the page along with your fax number. For some reason, you'll get three fax-backs for every phone call. Prospects are simply more comfortable using them as opposed to picking up the phone and calling you. See the sample flyer at the end of Chapter 14 for an example.

Keep all of these points constantly in mind as you take the remainder of this program and customize the individual techniques for yourself. Remember, I don't know what your product is, what your sales cycle is, anything about your company, or anything about you and your style of selling. You'll need to take the time to sit down, review the key points listed above and in other areas of this book, and figure out how to *creatively* apply them to your product or service. The key here is *creatively*. You can't do what everyone else is doing and expect success. Be creative and stand out from the crowd!

## Part 2: Never Cold Call... Unless Your Boss Says You Have To!

# Bridging The Gap from Cold Calling to Never Cold Calling Again

One of the nice things about NeverColdCall.com is that almost no one returns this program. Nearly everyone finds at least some benefit from it, well in excess of its modest cost.

However, of the few returns we do receive, they all give the same reason: "My boss says I have to cold call, so I can't use your system."

Likewise, as I've built my career as a professional speaker - the logical next step after becoming a best-selling author - I encountered a lot of resistance at first. Corporations didn't want to bring me in to train their sales reps. They figured that since I'm the "Never Cold Call Again" guy, I'd tell their reps not to make sales calls.

This is not the case at all, but unfortunately it's the perception that's out there.

In response to those challenges, as well as to popular demand for more information on what to do if your boss says you have to make cold calls, along with how to bridge the gap on your journey from cold calling to never cold calling again, this section of the course was written.

Along with that comes a lot of good news. For starters, when I wrote the very first version of this course way back in 2003, teaching people how to cold call effectively, if they must, wasn't an option. That's because the ability to make effective cold calls (again, if you must), is specifically the result of the growth of the Internet, and social media in particular. Although there is a separate section of this course dedicated to social media, I'm going to show you some easy ways to use it in this section, in order to make a cold contact in such a way that you come in "under the radar" and prospects won't view you as an annoying cold caller.

Another bit of good news comes from the fact that these new strategies will give you a way to make a smooth transition to never cold calling again. When someone bought the first edition of this course in 2003, and even a few years thereafter, it was a difficult transition to make. They had to go directly from cold calling, to my never cold call strategies that are detailed in Part 3 of the course.

This of course meant that they had to continue cold calling, while also managing to build the never cold call strategies, in order to keep the lead flow coming in. There was no way around it.

Now I'm going to give you methods of using the Internet and social media that will allow you to instantly stop cold calling, start connecting with high-value prospects in an indirect way that won't trigger sales resistance, and will start getting you easy sales as you start to work on the never cold call strategies.

So with that in mind, let's get to it!

# Never Make A "Cold Call" - Make Informed Calls

The very first thing you need to do, whether your cold calling the bad old way, or in the new effective way I'm about to show you, is to have a list of target prospects.

Cold calling is bad enough, but when you're calling people completely at random, with absolutely no idea of whether they need what you have, or if they're even a desirable prospect, you're just digging yourself into a deeper hole.

With my "how to cold call if you have to" strategy, or even with bad old traditional cold calling, the very first step in an effective sales process is to compile a list of desirable prospects.

If you're in business-to-business sales, this is a no brainer. You know what the profile of an ideal customer is. You know who the businesses in your community are (or you should, anyway). You have easy access via the Internet to find and learn about target prospects. So there's no excuse for you to skip this step.

If you're in business-to-consumer sales, it's a bit trickier, but can still be done. For example, real estate agents should be reading the announcements in local newspapers of marriages and births. Now that the housing bubble of the 2000s is over, we're back to the way things used to be: People buy a house when they get married. So new marriage announcements are prime prospects.

Announcements of promotions in your local Business Journal is another great source. These are people who just received an increase in income, which means easier qualifying for a loan, or the desire to finally buy that first home, or upgrade to a bigger one. This also goes for anyone in any type of luxury sales - home theater, alarm systems, cars, and so on.

Likewise, a life insurance agent should be looking for the same types of announcement, with marriages and births in particular. The birth of a child really brings the need and importance of life insurance to the forefront of one's mind. So target new parents, instead of people at random.

You should have a good solid list of 50 - 100 target prospects. Once that's done, it's time to start doing some homework.

## The Research Phase, Part 1

The first thing you need to do is learn about each company and find out who the decision makers are (if you're in B2C sales, you can skip this step, because the prospect himself is obviously the decision maker).

The best way to do this is online, right on the company's website. The "About" section of practically any site will have a section about who the staff and management are.

You can also find this on LinkedIn and Facebook. LinkedIn is easy - just search for the company and look at the results. If they're on LinkedIn, you'll see all of the management in search results.

Facebook is different, but still easy: If it's a small business, 9 times out of 10 the owner of the business is the one doing the Facebook posts. Larger companies will either have an employee doing that work, or will outsource it altogether to a social media firm, making things trickier.

## The Research Phase, Part 2

Now for the fun part - you get to learn all about your target prospect, in this case a specific decision maker!

This is easier than it sounds, and there is a lot more information available than you would imagine. Your sources: Facebook, LinkedIn, and Twitter. You'll also want to do a Google search to find out if the individual has a blog. If so, all the better.

The trick here is to look for *personal* details - something you can use to make a personal connection. This makes it a lot easier to initiate contact and get things rolling. Look for information like where they went to school, what their hobbies are, if they have kids or pets, where they like to travel, and so on.

The sheer volume of information you can glean by doing this is really astounding, and honestly it's quite scary. Here is just some of what anyone can learn about me by reading my Facebook and LinkedIn profiles along with my Twitter feed:

- I'm married

- I'm a dad

- I am a Great Dane owner

- I'm a ham radio operator

- I'm a shooting sports enthusiast

- I'm a wine and cigar lover

- I'm a foodie

- I'm a car detailing fanatic

- I'm a huge major Rush fan

- I read Napoleon Hill on an ongoing basis

- What kind of car I drive

- What my previous cars were

- My wife & kids' names

- My dog's name

- What kind of cigars I like

- What kind of wine I like and what wine clubs I belong to

- What kind of food I like

- All the places I've lived

- Who my friends are

- Who my family is

- Where I went to school

- Awards and accolades I've won

- Where I've vacationed

- Where I get my coffee every day

- Where I go to lunch

- What magazines I read

- Who my favorite authors are

- What my favorite movies and TV shows are

...and so on and so on! You can even see what kinds of appliances I have in my kitchen, what my backyard looks like, and other fine details from looking at photos on Facebook and Twitter.

Not many salespeople are doing this kind of social research, but the ones who are are miles ahead of the rest. I can tell you that when someone contacts me to chat about my dog or child or hobbies, or cigars or wine, I'm a lot more inclined to take the call or write back than when I receive a regular cold call.

Now that you're armed with this information, you're ready to move on to the next step - befriending your prospects via social media. But before going on to that chapter, I want to let you know that it's not a required step. It is a very effective way to come in "under the radar," but if you uncover something in your research that gives you enough confidence to pick up the phone or send a direct message on LinkedIn, then by all means do it. For example, anyone who falls into the category of huge Rush fan or ham radio operator would be fine contacting me directly, and they would know it, because these are two communities of people with a strong connection.

For all the rest of your prospects, for whom you haven't found any big triggers or connections, the next chapter is for you.

# Forget About Prospects.
# Make Friends Instead.

The advent of social media has made my career as an author & speaker a lot more satisfying, for the fact that I have a lot more connections and even friendships with people who started out as readers and fans.

In the past, the gatekeeper and elaborate voicemail trickery prevented anyone from reaching me on the phone, and replies to emails were limited and guarded.

However, many people have made direct connections with me by friending me on Facebook and showing a real interest in my own personal interests, or by connecting on LinkedIn and recommending me or otherwise gaining my interest.

This isn't all that hard to do, even with high-profile people. When people ask me how on earth I've been backstage at Rush concerts, a band with notoriously tight security, I explain that I simply made a conscious effort to befriend their head of security. I found out what kind of cigarettes and whisky he likes, and began sneaking it in. I got his email address and started giving him a heads-up that I'm on my way, which finally results in driving right into the coveted backstage area, whisky and smokes in hand, and parking right next to the drummer's Aston Martin & motorcycle trailer.

Now I have a nice collection of drumsticks, a hand-written thank you note from the drummer himself for my "gifts," and some great stories and memories such as watching a soundcheck from behind the stage.

This same type of strategy can be used in sales, very easily, and to great effect.

The first thing you'll want to do is connect on LinkedIn, add as a friend on Facebook, and follow on Twitter. If there's also a Facebook fan page, you can like it as well.

Next, take an interest in the person's posts. Remember all that research you did looking for common ground? There's so much information available that it's nearly impossible not to find something you can connect on. If you're both dog owners, comment on photos of their dogs. "Like" photos of their kids - as a parent myself, I can tell you this is almost a too-easy way to win someone over.

If it's a major prospect, or a very highly-desired one, take your time. Don't be too obvious. Do it gradually, and win their favor over time. This is how fans of mine have converted to friends, and how I began parking backstage at Rush. It took time. Smaller prospects, or those who make themselves more available and easier to reach, will be much faster and easier to work.

## Making the Contact

Before shooting an email off or picking up the phone, I want to explain the social dynamic at work in an initial sales contact, and how to use it to your advantage.

The best way I can explain it is with an example I read in an article recently, about how empowered women have become in modern society, and that it's now just as common for women to ask men out on dates as for men to approach women.

The important thing, though, is that women report that they're far more attracted to men they approach, then to men who approach them!

This is particularly interesting because it flies in the face of common opinion on the subject, but it actually makes a lot of sense when you look at the psychology behind it.

The reality is that people put a higher value on anything they can't seem to have, or anything that's harder to get.

They key word here is seem. It's all about perception. The fact of the matter is that the man may have been about to get up and approach the woman, but because she did it first, he seems to be more desirable, and of higher value. For all we know, he may have done nothing more than position himself to where the woman would notice him, and hopefully make an approach.

And this is exactly what you need to do in befriending prospective customers with social media. What you're doing is making yourself seen, in a favorable light. This isn't being phone or disingenuous; it's smart business in a world where cold calling is neither effective nor tolerated anymore. This is especially true if the prospect will benefit from your product or service. How else will they know about you if they won't take cold calls?

This is why you lay groundwork first and gain favor. Once that's done, you can make the connection and set the appointment. Here are a few ways to go about it:


- If you and the prospect have established a strong connection, send a direct message online saying something to the effect of, "Hey, this is what I do, and from looking at your business, I think you'd really benefit from it."

- You can pick up the phone and say, "Hey, this is Frank, your Facebook friend - I wanted to give you a ring to actually talk in person."

- Offer to buy the prospect lunch at his or her favorite lunch spot. You do know where that is by now, don't you?


This should give you enough food for thought to get started. Be creative. Your job is no longer that of salesperson - it's the job of a connector.

One of the most successful people I know in business almost literally knows everyone in his city, and he's a transplant - he's not even from there! When I asked him how he did it, he said after relocating, he spent the first few months networking nonstop. He went to a breakfast networking meeting every weekday morning, he went to a networking happy hour every weekday evening, and we went out to a karaoke bar in the city's central business district a few nights a week, where he knew he'd have a good time - with the city's movers & shakers.

This sounds like a lot of work, and it was, but it was also well over ten years ago. Now that you have endless social media at your fingertips, you can network that well - or even better - without leaving the comfort of your home or office.

# Never Tell Them What You Can Do. Show Them.

At one of my first outside sales jobs, at a large Fortune 500 corporation, we were taught in sales training to go door-to-door in office buildings and business parks, ask for a decision maker, and start out with, "We can help your business."

I'd been at this for about 2 days when I got a really rude awakening, in the form of a prospect who got in my face and told me, on no uncertain terms and in an angry voice, that I can't help him, that he could help me by giving me a sale, but that I really could not help him.

He was partially right.

I was selling a quality service that would've put some lost money back in his pocket, but he had no way of knowing that. Jaded prospects like him don't want to be told what you can do for them - they want to be shown.

## A Huge Advertising Sale

About a year ago I was approached by an online advertising account executive. I almost automatically refuse these contacts because I've lost huge amounts of money on online advertising that doesn't work, but this approach was a bit different.

Instead of asking to set up a call or an appointment, she merely asked a few very basic questions that took me under a minute to answer via email (I hate scheduling calls and almost never do it unless I can see huge value in it for me). The rest of the information she needed was readily available online from various sources - sound familiar?

She got back to me a couple of weeks later with an extremely detailed proposal, showing exactly how much return on investment I'd see, based on my real-life marketing data gleaned from the Internet. I saw the value, and scheduled the call.

We did a GoToMeeting and she presented a very handsome PowerPoint to me, explaining everything that was in the proposal but in further detail.

A year later I spend over $40,000 per month with this provider, and she's getting a nice residual commission each month with minimal work or follow-up.

Now what happened there? It's important to consider because it flies in the face of typical sales logic, which says to make a cold call, then set an appointment for fact-finding, then come back with a proposal and try to close the sale.

In this case she didn't waste my time with that initial appointment, or even try to pester me to set up a call. She did her homework, and did it without bothering me.

And the result was a very nice sale for her, and a major increase in income for me, one that has allowed me to pump more money back into advertising, meaning even more revenue for her.

## A Suddenly Wealthy Web Designer

With the recent economic recession, many capable, educated people found themselves suddenly out of work. Someone I know ended up in this very situation, and decided to start a business, working from home, doing web design and local marketing for small businesses.

However, he didn't do the usual cold calling and advertising that web designers do. Instead, he did his homework and searched online for just about every local business he could find.

He noted the ones with especially bad websites - sites that either were amateurish looking, or that were not optimized for marketing.

He then went through them one by one, and created a stunning, effective, professional website, and uploaded it to his own hosting account.

The initial contact with each decision maker was simple: Via an email or a direct message on Facebook or LinkedIn, he wrote something to the effect of, "I'm a local web designer, and I recently came across your website and had some ideas on how to improve it. I've built an all-new website, that you can view at this link. If you like what you see, I can have it live and online in a matter of minutes for $_____. Just give me a call or write back to move forward."

His closing rate was over 90%.

The bottom line here?

He doesn't TELL prospects what he can do. He SHOWS them.


## A Top Real Estate Agent

Last month, in a casual meeting with a local real estate agent who was showing me around Dallas, he brought along a few samples of mailers he was considering, and asked for my expert opinion on which one to go with.

Naturally, I skipped all of the ones about how great he is and how helpful he'd be, and went directly for the one stating that he closed over $15 million last month.

That's not telling or making vague promised - that's showing real RESULTS.

I don't know what you happen to sell, and in fact the readers of my books are so diverse as far as industries go that you'd be completely amazed if I could list them all. But whatever it is, figure out how you can SHOW people results, rather than making vague promises and talking typical sales talk that no one believe anymore, nonsense like, "We have the best service."

Whether you can show results in advance like the web designer did, or whether you have to be more indirect and demonstrate results as the result of verifiable case studies, I can tell you that decision makers like myself are only interested in seeing results.

Once you combine the strategy of connecting with desirable prospects on social media, and then making that contact in the form of a demonstration of results, you will be unstoppable. And the best part is that you'll be flooded with so much referral business that you'll probably never have to prospect again.

## Part 3: The *Never Cold Call Again*® Lead-Generation System

# Using Flyers Properly:
# A Twist on Banging Doors

*"I spent an hour getting 50 flyers out today and 3 faxed
back already asking to meet with me."*

*- Frank Rumbauskas,
to a salesperson who spent 3 hours making 50
cold calls with nothing to show for it*

The very first and most basic "non-cold-calling" marketing technique I ever learned and used with great success is the concept of flyer distribution. This one threw me at first because it seemed too simple to possibly work, and because it closely resembles cold calling.

To understand why it's decidedly different than cold calling, let's take a look at the definition of the term "cold calling" as found on dictionary.com: "Cold calling": The ethically questionable practice of making unsolicited calls to people one doesn't know in order to attract new business.

Wow. "Ethically questionable." If that's the new dictionary definition of cold calling, what does that say about the legitimacy of cold calling in our modern-day, Information Age society? In any case, I've already devoted enough of this book to explaining why cold calling is dead so I won't dwell on it here.

The idea of distributing flyers came to me as a result of the limited amount of direct mail I had been doing at the time. I figured the same piece simply dropped off at a prospect's office would be more effective because whoever received it would get to see the message right away, without the filter of an envelope and the high probability that it would get thrown away without ever being opened like most junk mail is. In addition, distributing the pieces in person would allow me to get in the office and pick up a business card containing contact information without generating all the resistance and negative connotations that go along with making an actual cold call. The game plan was to walk in, hand my information over, grab a card, and leave without saying anything other than "Hi, here you are, have a great day." No cold calling. No selling. No pissing anyone off. No getting thrown out or hearing those dreaded words, "No soliciting!"

Guess what? It worked! In a typical day of cold calling fifty doors, I would spend about three hours and usually get no leads, or maybe one if I was lucky. By contrast, I could hand out fifty flyers in less than an hour and would average two or three leads a day as a result!

The results were great enough that I devoted more time to it. Instead of spending an hour getting fifty flyers out, I could spend two hours distributing a hundred flyers and therefore double the amount of leads generated in a day. It worked. My flyers included a fax-back form, as yours should, and I'd come home after a couple of hours of passing out flyers to find three or four leads sitting on the fax machine, ready and waiting for me.

At this point I was starting to put the power of leverage to work for me. I effectively tripled the amount of contacts I made. Instead of spending three hours making fifty contacts, I could make three times that amount in the same time period. In addition, my effective rate of contact increased exponentially and here's why. A cold call is an intangible event that takes place and once it's over, it's over.  You get the brush-off and it's gone forever.  With a flyer however, I was leaving something tangible behind.  Instead of being gone in an instant, it was placed on the decision maker's desk or in his or her inbox.  Can you see why this is so effective?  Most direct mail never makes it to the decision maker's desk.  On the other hand, a well-written and well-designed flyer will almost always make it to the decision maker's desk.  That's why a response rate of 1% is considered good in direct mail and is about what one can expect from cold calling.  My flyers, however, consistently returned a 5% response rate over time.

Now that I was starting to experience the power of leverage, I wanted even more.  Instead of tying up my own time spending a few hours a day passing out flyers, I opened up the yellow pages and looked for a flyer distribution company.  I knew there had to be several judging solely by the amount of menus and flyers from pizza shops I found hanging on my doorknob every night when I came home.  Sure enough, I found one offering a great deal.  Their pricing was $350 for a 5,000 flyer distribution or $600 for a 10,000 flyer distribution, including a fax at the close of every business day with a map showing what specific areas they hit.  Just think of it – 5% of 5,000 calling me, pre-qualified and ready to buy!  I didn't hesitate.  I went with the cheaper option, plunked down my $350, and I was put on the schedule for a few weeks later.

The day came and my flyer distribution started.  Immediately, my fax machine began to fill up with completed fax-back forms from prospects who where very interested in what I had to offer.  At the end of the first month, I had received *over fifty qualified leads!*  By contrast, in a great month of cold calling I was fortunate to find ten!  (Keep in mind that I was selling business telephone systems, something a typical business only buys once every ten years on average.  It's not an easy product to prospect for.)

Every city and town has at least one flyer distribution service.  First, check your yellow pages.  If you don't find one there, ask around.  Visit your local pizza shop and find out who distributes their flyers and door hangers.  Chances are you'll be able to find a great deal like I did and immediately put it to work for you.

Mass flyer distribution gives you a tremendous amount of leverage.  That first month, I received fifty qualified leads from my flyers alone.  Compare that to what I generated consistently as a result of cold calling several hours a day, every day:  ten qualified leads in a month.  I had effectively multiplied my power by five.  It was like having five of me out beating the streets every day, full-time, day in and day out.  The best part was that I had once and for all eliminated cold calling from my life!

This is the easiest, simplest, and cheapest way for a salesperson to immediately jump-start their sales, start bringing in big numbers, and take the first step towards forever getting cold calling out of their lives.

You'll find a sample flyer on the following page.  This is the real, actual flyer I used over three years ago when I was running a telecom sales agency.  It doesn't look like much, but it was supremely effective – so much so that I continue to get calls today from people who still find them lingering around their offices!  It's a prime example of how something that appears so deceptively simple can actually be hugely effective.

One thing to keep in mind with flyers:  the effects are definitely cumulative.  It will take some time before the calls start pouring in consistently, but believe me, they will.  It's very important to use your own personal number (usually a cell number) as well as your own fax number (such as an eFax.com number) for this reason.  If you change jobs, you want to make sure you continue to get those calls, not your old company.  I learned that lesson the hard way, so be sure to do it!

# HIGH-SPEED INTERNET AVAILABLE *NOW* AT *YOUR* LOCATION - CALL (602)555-5555

We represent over a dozen of Arizona's high-speed Internet providers. We'll provide you with information and pricing on *every* service available at your location and let *you* choose.  No more high-pressure, heavily biased sales pitches from pushy Internet and telecom salespeople!

- Services available in ALL areas
- Wired and wireless services available
- Flexible plans to suit all business needs and budgets
- We also offer networking, LAN and WAN, wireless networks, and computers at deep-discount prices
- We also offer the best prices on local phone service, T1, PRI

## *AGGRESSIVE PROMOTIONS ON BUSINESS TELEPHONE SYSTEMS - LUCENT/AVAYA, NEC, AND CISCO SYSTEMS*

The slow economy is resulting in the best pricing and leasing deals ever on new business telephone systems.  Call for a free consultation, site survey, and quote on a new phone system or upgrade.  We also do complete wire and cabling services.

## CALL (602)555-5555  TODAY, OR FAX BACK TO (602)000-0000:

*Name*_____*Company*_____

*Telephone* _____*Best time to call*_____

*Interested in* _____

*We currently have:*

_____

*Or, Email Me Today:  Frank Rumbauskas    frank@nevercoldcall.com*
*Hurry and take up this special offer to save today!*

## Flyers – Action Items

- Sit down and create a good one-page flyer based on the principles discussed in the chapter "How to Succeed in Sales." Include your main contact information and be sure to have a simple fax-back form on the page along with your fax number in bold print.

- Immediately start spending the time you normally devote to cold calling on getting your flyers out. Remember, this will typically triple the amount of qualified leads you're able to generate in a given amount of time. What's more, you enticed them to call you and so the positive frame of BUYING is set right from the start, instead of the negative frame of SELLING.

- In your spare time, seek out a flyer distribution service. If you can't find one in the yellow pages, search online. Pizza shops are a great place to ask because nearly all of them employ flyer distribution companies to litter the world with their door-hangers and menus.

- The power of leverage is working for you. Follow these instructions and you'll multiply your power by five.

# Dialing for Dollars.  My way.

*"Any mistakes you commit through audacity are easily corrected with more audacity.  Everyone admires the bold; no one honors the timid"*

*- Robert Greene and Joost Elffers, "The 48 Laws of Power"*

Let me start by saying that I think the phone is a very, very powerful tool in selling.  Proper use of the telephone is essential in effective prospecting.

What?  Mr. Never Cold Call is advocating the use of the telephone to prospect?  That's right.  But the key words here are *proper* and *effective*.

Few salespeople use the telephone properly.  As you read these examples of typical telephone sales calls, think about whether or not they would make you want to meet with the person on the other end of the line:

- "Hello, Mr. Customer.  This is Frank Rumbauskas with FJR Advisors, Inc.  We help businesses just like yours become more profitable.  It just so happens that I'll be in your neighborhood next Tuesday meeting with other companies like yours.  How about 10am?  Does that work for you?"

- "Hi, this is Frank over at FJR Advisors, Inc.  I have some ideas that can help your business and I'd like to get together with you.  Is Wednesday at 10am or Thursday at 2pm better?  Which one would you like to go with?"

- "Hi, this is Frank Rumbauskas.  We can save you money on your local telephone, long-distance, and Internet bills.  When can I stop by for fifteen minutes to review your bills and find out how much we can save you?"

Chances are, you've used or are currently using pitches like these yourself.  I'm especially uncomfortable with some of the sleazier tactics out there, such as "would tomorrow at 2 or the following day at 10 be better?"  How would you like people calling you up on the phone, trying to pull that on you?  Or how about "you wouldn't want to miss out in a great opportunity, would you?"  In my opinion, questions like those are beyond sleazy – they're downright unethical. (Keep that definition of cold calling from the previous chapter in mind.)

Once I had my flyers going full-force, I was getting plenty of leads but it bothered me that I still had quality prospect lists and stacks of business cards full of good contact information sitting around collecting dust.  However, I wasn't about to start calling them myself – I knew from experience that doing so would be a waste of time, not to mention the fact that I absolutely hate cold calling on the phone and didn't need to anyway thanks to all my flyer-generated leads.

I finally came up with a creative use for the information.  Go back and read the examples of typical telephone cold calls one more time.  Now, read the following examples.  Which ones would get you to agree to a meeting?

- "Hello, this is so-and-so. I work as an executive assistant to Mr. Frank Rumbauskas in his office. It appears Mr. Rumbauskas has thirty minutes available on his schedule tomorrow afternoon that I'd like to put you down for if you should be available as well."

- "Hi, is this Mr. Bigshot's secretary? Great. I'm an assistant to Mr. Rumbauskas here at FJR Advisors. I'm calling to schedule a thirty minute meeting between him and Mr. Bigshot."

Can you see the difference? Can you see how UNBELIEVABLY EFFECTIVE these examples would be, especially the second one?

The key is not to make phone calls yourself, but rather to have someone pose as your assistant and set appointments for you. Heck, at this point they're not even posing. That person really IS your assistant.

This is easier to accomplish than you may think. You may know someone who can do this for you. Perhaps a spouse, child, friend or cousin who doesn't work full-time or is in college and has an hour or two during the day to spend making your phone calls. If you don't know anyone, contract telemarketers are plentiful. I've typically paid $10-15/hour plus a small spiff for each appointment set. With a usual minimum of 10 hours, for a small initial investment you can have your "executive assistant" setting appointments for you with otherwise inaccessible decision makers and executives. Keep in mind you'll be getting through and getting face-to-face meetings with the people who normally never meet with salespeople, ever. Be sure to review the information on power and image before meeting with these people. You must be totally congruent with it and carry it all the way through to the end, and I mean to the end. If not, it will backfire on you.

Another great way to use your appointment setter is to have that person follow up on a very nice, professional letter you may have sent out in advance. The typical mailer or literature follow-up call goes something like this:

- "Hello Mrs. Customer, this is Frank with FJR Advisors, Inc. Did you get the information we sent out to you last week?"

Obviously, this gives all the power away to the prospect. Even if they did get it, they can say they didn't as a quick and easy way to get rid of you. Now let's contrast that with the call your assistant is going to make:

- "Hello Mrs. Customer, this is so-and-so, executive assistant to Mr. Frank Rumbauskas. I'm calling to schedule an appointment between yourself and Mr. Rumbauskas to discuss the points covered in the letter you recently received from us."

Again, see the difference? The first example is needy and is essentially asking the prospect for permission to speak. In addition, the call is made by the salesperson himself which creates the impression that he's needy, is trying to scrape up business, and has nothing else going on that particular day.

The second example comes from a position of power. First of all, it's from the salesperson's "executive assistant." This creates an immediate and strong impression that the salesperson is a busy, powerful executive who's out doing important things, not sitting around the office making cold calls. Secondly, no questions are asked. The caller never asks if the mailer was received, or if they may set a time to meet. The caller clearly states the following: "You received our mailer." (This drastically cuts down on the possibility that the prospect will deny having received it.) "I'm calling to set an appointment for him to meet with you." (Again, we're not asking for anyone's permission. We're setting a frame that an appointment is going to take place no matter what and the only thing left to decide is when.)

Do this. Now. Go back and read the quote at the beginning of this chapter and always remember that everyone admires the bold and no one admires the timid. Audacity works. Power and perception are everything. Reality that is not seen counts for nothing.

## Telephone – Action Items

- Don't spend time on the phone setting your own appointments. Prospects will see you as being needy and as having nothing better to do with your time.

- Get someone to do your appointment setting for you. This increases your leverage and paints a picture of you as a busy, important, powerful executive who has too many important things going on in your life. You don't have time to make phone calls.

- Having someone else act as your assistant and schedule your appointments on your behalf will get you meetings with the prime, elusive prospects who normally will not meet with unsolicited salespeople under any circumstance.

- If you don't have a friend, spouse, or relative with a spare hour or two during the day, contract telemarketers are readily available, are effective, and charge very reasonable fees that will more than justify the investment.

- Having your appointment setter follow up on a professional sales letter, when done properly, increases your chances of getting the appointment and significantly reduces the probability of being turned down.

- The amazing power of leverage continues to multiply exponentially in your favor. Your flyer program multiplied your power by five. These phone techniques at least twice as powerful as you can be on your own. You now have seven times your original prospecting power working for you.

# E-Mail for Hot Leads

*"I wouldn't be sitting around chin-wagging if I were you. There are plenty of six-figure names in that zip code file to cold call."*

*- Bud Fox's sales manager in "Wall Street"*

E-mail is one of the single most powerful weapons in the Information Age salesperson's arsenal, but the vast majority fail to use it. Salespeople who use it have a decided advantage over those who do not.

Here's an astounding fact: In my old days of cold calling I found that for every ten messages I left, I got one or two calls back, if I was lucky. Sometimes I got none. For every ten initial contacts I made via email, I'd typically get four or five replies back. What's more, even the ones who weren't interested would send back a polite reply saying something like, "Thanks for contacting us, we don't have any need for that at this time but we appreciate the information anyway."

What really frustrates me is that I tell salespeople this and yet the majority continue to insist on making phone calls themselves in an attempt to set appointments despite the fact that email gets a much higher and more positive response. I think it goes back to the fact that they've been programmed for so long that they cannot possibly imagine doing anything other than cold calling to generate leads. I can't tell you how many times I set an appointment via email and never had a regular voice conversation with the prospect until the actual meeting took place. In addition, I had a percentage of sales that took place with no conversations whatsoever. They happened entirely via email! You have to remember that a lot of people nowadays have gotten used to email and prefer it. I even remember a few times when I set appointments in order to satisfy some micro-manager who required a minimum number per day, and the prospect told me on no uncertain terms that they would have preferred to communicate via email and that I was wasting their valuable time by insisting on holding a face-to-face meeting.

IMPORTANT NOTE: Never, never, NEVER do anything that may be interpreted as wasting someone else's time.

The bottom line here is that prospects appreciate someone who respects their time. We've already covered in great detail the reasons why unsolicited telephone cold calls are annoying and disrespectful. Why, then, would anyone choose to do something that automatically stacks the odds against them when a better alternative is available? What's more, it's something that everyone already has access to, and it's FREE!

Block out fifteen or twenty minutes a day to send out follow-up emails. Cut & paste the same message and you'll get a ton out in a short amount of time. Also use the time to send email thank-you notes to the people you've already met with that day. Like everything else I teach, this sounds overly simple and too easy to work, but you will be amazed at the results. Keep an open mind and try it.

## E-Mail – Action Items

- Don't blow your chances of getting an appointment by calling yourself. Follow up with an email first.

- The response rate of email is 3-5 times better than the callback rate associated with leaving phone messages. Don't lock yourself into "voice mail jail" when the freedom and ease of email is readily available to you.

- Email is free. Everyone has it. It instantly puts your message in front of the prospect. Why use the phone when you already have something this good at your fingertips?

- Your leverage is increasing explosively. Add another factor of two into the mix by using these simple email techniques and your power is now multiplied by nine. A month of consistent use of these methods together will yield as many leads as nine months of cold calling.

# Don't Let Them Forget You

*"Being in the right place at the right time won't cut it anymore.*
*You must find ways to be in all places at all times."*

*- Frank Rumbauskas,*
*on how the Information Age has forever changed the game of selling*

One of the keys to success in our new Information Age economy that is important to remember is the fact that in order to succeed, or even survive for that matter, you must find ways and means of being in all places at all times. You must continually come at your prospects from all angles and at different times. You must use the element of surprise and catch them off-guard.

An easy, free way to do this that you can get started on immediately is to write your own online newsletter. This doesn't have to be anything fancy or showy. A simple text email with some bullet-points will do for now.

Remember how we talked about the power of emailing prospects rather than using the phone? An email newsletter lets you leverage that same power but in a different way, in keeping with the theme of hitting your prospects from as many different angles as possible.

The content of your newsletter must contain some information that is beneficial to your prospects. A shameless sales pitch sent out once a month isn't going to get you anywhere. Think of something in your industry or some way in which you can provide useful information to your prospects that will keep them interested in your newsletter and get them to read it whenever it comes in.

Here are some useful examples of real email newsletters I've seen different types of salespeople use with great success:

- Realtors can provide useful information on property values, tips for first-time buyers, updates on mortgage rates, changes in real estate law, etc.

- Financial services salespeople provide tips on reducing tax liability, protecting estates from unfair taxation, free investment advice, etc.

- As a salesman of broadband Internet and network services, I provided free information on Internet security, e-commerce, Internet marketing, and other Internet-related topics of interest to prospects. When the time came to buy these services, guess who they called?

An especially powerful way to accomplish a newsletter is through the use of an autoresponder system. This is simply a series of newsletter emails that you write in advance and save into the system. Whenever you add an email address to the list, the system automatically begins sending out your preset series of emails in the order you specify. You can even set the time interval between emails and change them at will. The system also lets you send out broadcast messages to your entire list whenever you want, which is useful for keeping your prospects updated with the latest information, or perhaps to send holiday greetings to your list as they come up. This, in fact, is how the nevercoldcall.com free newsletter works. One great service is by www.aweber.com and I highly recommend it to others. The cost is very modest at $19.95/month and the site even includes detailed instructions and tips on how to use it most effectively. They even provide instructions on how to put a sign-up form on your website that automatically adds new email addresses to your list as people join.

As you can see, a free email newsletter keeps you and your message in the prospect's mind at all times, with no exceptions whatsoever. If they've received your newsletter on a regular basis, and especially if they gained some useful knowledge from it, chances are they'll call or email you when the time comes to buy whatever product or service it is that you have to offer. What's more, chances are you're the only one who will get the call and your competition will be left out in the cold. They'll be the ones who waste their time making a cold call a few weeks later and hear "Oh, we just bought that from someone else, sorry."

One of the newest and most exciting things to come along recently, something that I'm implementing myself, is video email. The response rates are absolutely astounding. The statistics from regular old mass email (a.k.a. spam) state that regular text or html email gets less than a 1% clickthrough rate, while video email is getting over a 30% clickthrough rate! (Clickthrough rate simply means how many people read the email, then click on the link to the company's website.)

The uses for video email can be really fun and creative. It's so very personalized, especially to a prospect who may have already met you in person at one time or another. And if they haven't yet met you and eventually do, they tend to be much more enthusiastic during appointments. They feel as if they know you personally on some level just because they've seen you on video talking to them.

You'll be absolutely blown away by the response rates you'll get using video email! Here are the two ways I like to use it:

1. As an initial introduction. By sending an individual email, you can use the prospect's name and really get their attention. This is GREAT for higher-level executives or people who are hard to reach in general. It works – I've personally been sold by someone who used video email to make the initial contact. It really, really got my attention and stood out from the usual blur of advertising, spam, and cold calls.

2. As part of your ongoing newsletter or autoresponder series. A great way to do this is to include a short video greeting (less than one minute), followed by the actual text of your newsletter. One thing that works particularly well is to touch on the topic of the email. Say something like, "This newsletter touches on an important topic, _____, so think about how it applies to you while reading, and feel free to give me a call with any questions."

To get started, all you need is a webcam and a subscription to a video email service. The services are inexpensive (starting around $20/month) and a good quality webcam can now be purchased quite inexpensively as well. It's a small investment that will produce huge sales results for you, and really make you stand out from the rest of the competition.

Video email services can be found by searching online. You may want to consider using one that offers an affiliate program, since a lot of the people who receive your emails will be so impressed that they'll want to sign up too. After all, that's how I got started using it!

## A free newsletter – without the work!

I hear the following complaint a lot from salespeople when I tell them a free email newsletter is a must-have in today's marketplace:

*"But I don't want to write! I can't write! I don't have time to write!"*

As much as I highly recommend writing your own articles – writing is a wonderful way to gather your thoughts, develop your mind, and possibly even get a book published like myself and so many others have by collecting our thoughts over time – there is a way around having to write your newsletter yourself.

I'm talking about 'free reprint articles.' Free reprint articles can be found all over the net. One site I particularly like, and that I write for, is ezinearticles.com. You can find dozens of others by doing a Google search for 'free reprint articles.'

Free reprint articles are just that – articles that you can reprint for free without having to secure any special permission from the author or publisher. All you are required to do is print the article unchanged and include the author's bio, provided with the article, along with it.

And that brings me to another objection I get from salespeople:

*"I don't want to give the author's contact information!*
*My prospects will buy from them instead of me if I do!"*

Wrong again. Your prospects are not going to call the author of the article to buy. They're going to call YOU when the time comes. Here are the reasons why this works to your advantage:

1. You'll avoid reprinting any articles from local authors who also happen to be your competitors. Make sure the articles you reprint come from out-of-state authors. This will not be a problem because there are hundreds of thousands of free reprint articles available online, and at least several hundred from your particular industry. (Don't believe me? Go to ezinearticles.com right now and do a search for terms related to your industry. You'll be amazed at how many articles come up.)

2. Your newsletter comes from you every month (or week, or whatever). It is YOUR name that is constantly kept in front of your prospects. They think of you and will want to call YOU when the time comes, not the author of an article that appeared only once in your newsletter.

3. By printing articles by other authors, you actually increase your status as a business equal. How? Because it takes a certain amount of self-confidence to print articles from someone who might possibly be a competitor. Remember when I explained why prospects want to do business with salespeople who appear not to need any more business? This is exactly what your doing by printing someone else's article. The prospect thinks, "Wow, if he is willing to print an article from a potential competitor, he must really be doing well. He doesn't need my business. Therefore, I want to buy from him."

So, if you need content from your newsletter and don't want to write your own, or if you have written some articles but not enough to fill a monthly newsletter, go download some free reprint articles and put together the best damn newsletter your prospects have ever seen – then sit back and wait for them to call!

## Don't Let Them Forget You – Action Items

- Save all your prospects' email addresses as a group in your email program. Add new ones as you get them from business cards, from your website, or any other source.

- Put together a regular email newsletter that shares some information or knowledge that may be of benefit to your prospects.

- Avoid turning your newsletter into a blatant sales pitch. Rather, give them some helpful information then wrap up by reminding them of what you do and providing your contact information.

- Prospects who would've forgotten about you months before after a cold call will call YOU when they're ready to buy your product.

- Video email has become the most powerful form of keeping in touch of all. Use it, and your response rates will skyrocket.

- Don't want to write your own content? You don't have to – there are thousands of free reprint articles on the Internet, free for you to use.

- Your leverage goes up some more. Add another point to the total. By using all these techniques explained thus far together, you've multiplied your prospecting power by ten. It's like having ten full-time salespeople out there prospecting for you.

# More Fun With E-mail

*"It's all about bucks, kid. The rest is conversation."*

*- Gordon Gekko*

In my last full-time sales position selling broadband Internet services, I was consistently at 150-200% of quota. Another salesman in the office was also consistently at 150-200% of quota.

That's where our similarities ended.

He was what I like to call a "seven-to-seven" guy. He was always in the office by 7am, and almost never went home at night before 7pm.

I'm not a morning person and so my day usually started between 9am and 10am. I almost never worked past 4pm, especially during summer when the pool was waiting for me after a hot day in the field.

I was consistently at 150-200% of quota with that schedule. So was he.

He spent his day cold calling, beating the streets, pounding the pavement, dialing for dollars, and all the usual antiquated Industrial Age selling techniques.

I sat in the air conditioned office, sent out email, answered the phone and replied to the emails I got back, faxed or emailed contracts back and forth, and made those numbers without breaking a sweat.

How?

Email!

Using the power of mass email to send out your message will get results beyond your wildest dreams. At this time I had just discovered the power of email and was astonished at the results. I was literally working part-time and matching or beating out the sales reps who worked double-time. What more could you ask for?

Okay, let's get down to how I did it.

First of all, you need to write the content of your email ad with the guidelines listed in the chapter entitled "How to Succeed in Sales" always in mind. Find a niche and fill it. Find a unique angle to get their attention. Here's the exact email I used to market the Internet services I was selling:

**Subject: High Speed Internet now available at your location:**

**You'll be pleased to learn that high-speed Internet service is now available at your location, with a 1-2 week installation time! Our service is fully dedicated with a 99.97% uptime guarantee so you won't experience the slowdowns and outages that are so common with DSL.**

**Our current monthly pricing is as follows:**

**<prices were listed here>**

**You can reach me at the number below or simply reply to this email. We hope to serve you soon – thanks!**

**Frank Rumbauskas**
**\<phone number\>**
**\<address\>**

Okay, I know what you're thinking: this is spam. It is not. Let's look at the accepted definitions of "SPAM" vs. legitimate commercial email:

- SPAM: Generally is not a legitimate, useful business offer. Does not come from an actual valid email address. Does not contain a valid company name, valid address and valid telephone number.

- Legitimate commercial email (UCE): Is promoting a valid offer of interest to the recipient. Comes from a valid, reply-to email address. Contains a valid company name along with contact information including address and telephone number. Includes an option to be removed from the mailing list.

If you're concerned about illegitimate SPAM complaints to your Internet provider, there are many options available as far as 3rd party mass email companies go that will keep you and your email account immune from SPAM complaints. A quick Google search will reveal plenty of them. I recommend AWeber.com.

Where to get the emails? There are several options. Here are a few you can get started with right away:

- Chamber of Commerce websites now include online member directories complete with email addresses. This is a quick and easy way to start sending your message out today.

- Searching on Yahoo or another web directory for business in your area will yield big results. You can find the websites of literally hundreds upon hundreds of businesses in your local area. Go to the contact page of each site to get the contact email address. This sounds tedious but this is EXACTLY how I got started and produced those big 200% sales numbers at my Internet job.

- Buying a list is an option although they're usually not cheap.

- Using a complete email service is a great idea if you've got the budget. For a reasonable fee, you can use a "list rental" service which means they're simply sending your email to an existing list. Typical prices are about $50 for 5,000 emails, $75 for 10,000, etc. **NOTE**: Sending out this many emails at a time will generate an overwhelming response. When you schedule when your emails will go out (Tuesday and Wednesday morning typically generate the highest response), block out one or full two days just to answer the phone and reply to emails.

As you can see, mass email is an easy, cheap, simple method of generating simply tremendous amounts of leads.

## CAN-SPAM Compliance

Many U.S. readers have contacted us since the "CAN-SPAM" law went into effect regarding the legality of using email as a method of prospecting.

In reality, the CAN-SPAM law actually *helps* legitimate emailers like ourselves and was really intended to curb the proliferation of "business opportunity" scams, pornography, prescription drugs, and other annoyances that are commonly promoted through the use of bulk email.

Following is a summary of the requirements you must meet to be CAN-SPAM compliant:

- Your email must be for a legitimate offer and not a scam or offer of pornography, prescription drugs, or other questionably legal products.

- You must identify yourself and/or your company name in the email.

- You must provide your physical or mailing address in the email, usually at the end.

- Your email must originate from a real email address that people can reply to (of course it does, since your ultimate goal is to get replies from interested prospects).

- You must provide remove instructions or include a link that recipients can click on to remove themselves from future mailings.

- You must comply with all remove requests and avoid sending any more emails to people who ask to be removed.

As you can see, compliance is very simple and really does help legitimate commercial email to continue. In addition, by using a third-party email service that is CAN-SPAM compliant, you don't have to worry about it in the first place. I recommend a service such as AWeber.com or ConstantContact.com for this purpose.

## More Fun With E-mail – Action Items

- Take the time you'd otherwise waste making cold calls to no avail and instead spend emailing prospects in your area.

- Write a clear, concise, to-the-point email based on the guidelines. Send it to the email addresses you uncover. You will get an immediate response.

- If you're ready to move things up to the next level, plan to invest $50-100 dollars with an email company sending your message out to a list targeted to your prospects. This alone is at least as powerful as ten salespeople on the street. Block out the entire day to answer the phone and the incoming emails you'll get as a result.

- Your prospecting and lead-generating power is now reaching astronomical levels.

- NOTE: At this point, if you're using all the techniques explained thus far, you may start to receive more leads than you have time to handle. A great idea at this point is to sell them to other salespeople or hand them over with an agreement to a fair commission split. It's found money.

# Cast Your Net on the Worldwide Prospecting Web

*"Smart Internet marketers are raking in cash and making millions of dollars, while the average salesperson is still cold calling and going broke. Why?"*

*- Frank Rumbauskas*

What's the first thing that comes to most people's minds when they hear the term Information Age?

That's right. The Internet.

But what part of the internet, specifically?

The World Wide Web.

Having a website is no longer a luxury or a "plus" in our new Information Age economy. It's an absolute necessity.

Yes, even for you.

Despite common beliefs to the contrary, it's now easier and cheaper than ever to get online and get your own website up and running.

It's like having an expanded version of your flyer up on the Internet, available 24 hours a day, 7 days a week, 365 days a year, where anyone who's searching for it can quickly and easily find it.

It's like casting a massive net and pulling in all the leads that willingly swim right into it.

Keep in mind that anyone who responds to your website is actively looking for you and wants to buy your product.

How to get started?

It's easy.

There are plenty of web hosting companies that offer complete domain name registration services, inexpensive web hosting, and even easy point-and-click software that will let you create your own professional looking website and have it online in a matter of hours.

Two fantastic sources for creating a very professional website quickly and easily are Intuit Websites and GoDaddy. You can build and host a great website for a little as $5-$8 per month - the amount of money most of us spend on overpriced coffee each day! The services are point-and-click, and you can really pack a lot of information - and sales copy - into a nice looking five page website.

You can include a lot in five pages. Here are some guidelines as to what to include in your five pages:

- Homepage, providing a general overview
- About Us page, giving a brief company overview (it's okay to include here because you have five pages to work with and anyone who doesn't want to read it can easily bypass it)
- A page describing the product or service you're offering, including the benefits available to your customers

- A second page providing more product information or detail

- A contact page, including your name, phone number (which should be on your homepage as well), address, and most importantly, email address because email is the preferred contact method of most web users. This is a GREAT place to instruct site visitors to send an email requesting to be added to your free newsletter, or to use the pre-made signup forms provided by services such as AWeber.com. Even if these people don't buy now, chances are they will sooner or later.

The initial cost to get started is about $9 for one year of domain name registration, plus $5-8 per month for the hosting.

That's around $14 to have your own very own professional website online, immediately.

If you want to produce a bigger effort or have a site with a bit more complexity as far as adding contact forms, audio clips, etc., our NeverColdCall.com website is a perfect example. Here is a breakdown of the costs associated with getting it up and running and generating traffic:

- Domain name registration:  $ 9
- Anonymous registration (for reducing spam): $9
- Website template from Template Monster:  $ 69
- Hosting account (monthly):  $ 10*

Total amount: $97

(*NeverColdCall.com is hosted on a large dedicated server due to our extremely high traffic volume and PCI Compliance requirements; however, as a salesperson or even a small business, a $10 hosting account is more than sufficient.)

Not bad, huh? Again, contrary to popular belief, it's cheaper and easier than ever before to get good quality, lead-generating website online almost immediately.

The next step, once you've got your website up, is to get traffic to it. It doesn't do you any good to have a website that nobody is visiting.

The first and easiest way is to include your personal web address on all of your marketing materials and on your business cards as well, if that's possible. Prospects who receive your flyer, mailers, faxes, or other materials who might not have responded otherwise may visit your website to learn more. A percentage of them will respond or, at the very least, sign up for your newsletter and keep the line of communication open.

(As you build up your newsletter subscription list, you almost want to feel sorry for your competition. You're locking up the prospects before they even have a chance to introduce themselves!)

The second way is through Internet search engines and directories, both the free and paid varieties. Most search engines and directories offer a free, manual submission option that will get you listed sooner than waiting for the search engines to eventually find you. A fantastic resource for information on how to accomplish this is SearchEngineWatch.com. We won't go into the specifics of how to submit to search engine directories here because the information changes so frequently and will probably be outdated by the time you read this. Go to

SearchEngineWatch.com, go to their Search Engine Submission Tips section, and read it. The site contains a vast amount of information on how search engines work, optimization tips, up-to-date information on paid listings, and a wealth of other information.

It's especially important to submit to the online directories. This is because search engines "crawl" the web, including directories, and find new sites via links. Having links on the various free directories pointing to your site is the quickest way to get listed on the major search engines. (Keep in mind that even with the best-laid plans, it can take up to a month before your site starts to appear in search engine listings.)

Would you like to get immediate traffic to your site? I'm talking in a few minutes? There are a variety of cheap, "pay-per-click" paid listing services online. These include Google AdWords, Microsoft Advertising, and many others. Again, the most up-to-date information can be found on SearchEngineWatch.com so we won't go into great detail here. Having said that, Google AdWords is probably the cheapest and easiest way to generate traffic. They charge only a $5 signup fee and from that point on, you only pay for "clickthroughs" to your site, and you set the maximum amount you're willing to pay. Having used various paid listing services, I can safely say that Google AdWords has generated more traffic than all the others combined, and at a very reasonable cost. With proper selection of keywords and writing a good ad (you only get two lines of text plus a title, so you have to keep it short and to the point), you can realistically stretch out $20 or $30 over a month and get quite a large number of site visitors for that amount. Keep in mind that these visitors are out searching SPECIFICALLY for what you're offering. It's like having qualified prospects cold calling YOU! It's an immediate source for those elusive call-in leads we all want so much!

Put this book down, get online, and get your website up tonight. Don't hesitate. This is yet another method of lead-generation that works automatically, all by itself, and quite effectively at that, with absolutely no effort from you other than the few hours it takes to get set up initially.

Something else you can use that's similar to a website but not really a website is a "Blog," short for weblog. It's really just a diary but has become a powerful sales & marketing tool as of late. If you want to see what a blog looks like, you can view mine at http://nevercoldcall.typepad.com

At the time of this writing, most blogs are free - there are several free services available that you can quickly find by searching for blogs online such as Wordpress, Tumblr, and more (more advanced blogging strategies are covered in the social media section of the course). What you need to do to make it sell is to get the web address to as many people as possible, typically through email, flyers, your newsletter, your website, and other methods. Send the link to everyone you know and tell them to pass it on to anyone they know who may be interested. Try to post at least a few times a week, and talk about things that are relevant to your prospects' business. Most important of all, have a sense of humor and make it fun to read! You'll notice that most of my blog posts tend to be smart-alecky and slapstick, at least compared to my other writings. Why? This is to keep people coming back on a regular basis! As with video email, prospects who are complete strangers will start to feel as if they know you on a personal level, and will be a lot more likely to pick up the phone and call you. Be sure to include ways to get in touch with you on your blog page – at a minimum, include your email address and a link to your website, and preferably an email signup form.

Are you now seeing why working smarter, not harder, truly is the key to sales success in the Information Age? Not to mention a lot more fun!

## Cast Your Net on the Worldwide Prospecting Web – Action Items

- Immediately put this book down, go to GoDaddy or Intuit Websites - or a similar service - and get started immediately on casting your huge prospecting net out in the World Wide Web.

- Register a domain name and purchase one of the inexpensive, easy-to-use do-it-yourself website packages that are available.

- Using the guidelines in this book and your existing marketing materials as an additional guide, point-and-click your way to a great looking website in only a couple of hours.

- Be sure to include an option for site visitors to subscribe to your email newsletter. Doing so will keep the line of communication open with those prospects, and will almost guarantee locking out your competitors.

- Post a blog and get as many visitors to it as possible. Use email, flyers, newsletters, and every other available option to drive visitors to it.

- Sit back and reap the rewards of this additional automatic lead generator you've established. It works day and night, 24x7, 365 days a year whether you choose to work or not.

- Your power is now reaching astronomical proportions. You have more leads and business coming in than you ever dreamed of. By now you've doubled your sales and are working less.

# Get Hot Leads with Free Seminars

*"Every battle is won before it's ever fought."*

*- Sun Tzu, "The Art of War"*

Would you like to have a captive audience of qualified prospects who are genuinely interested in what you have to say, and are already obligated to you by virtue of having shown up?

If you've ever wanted to gain some experience in public speaking, now is your time. If you're afraid of public speaking, take a class on it, join Toastmasters, and get over your fear so you can begin using this very powerful method of generating new business.

Inviting prospects to a free seminar is similar to your free email newsletter in many ways. You're providing them with useful, free information with no obligation. They're getting to know you in a setting other than a series of uncomfortable sales appointments. You're keeping the line of communication open so that even if they're not ready to buy your product now, when they are you'll be the first, and probably the only person they'll call. Best of all, you'll be seen as an impartial expert on the subject matter.

What? A salesperson? Impartial? How can that be?

When you provide free, useful, beneficial information to your prospects in your area of expertise, with no sales pressure or obligations or expectation that they'll buy attached to it, they'll forget that you're a salesperson and begin to see you as a knowledgeable expert in your respective industry. That's why they'll automatically be predisposed to buy from you and only you when the time comes.

When it comes to doing free seminars, start small. You don't want to spend much money your first time around because, after all, it's your first time and speaking in front of a group may not be something you're entirely comfortable with yet.

Most restaurants that are popular lunch spots in busy commercial or business areas have small rooms or seating areas that are at least semi-private and that can be reserved with no additional cost beyond the price of the meals. Call a few restaurants in your territory and you'll have no trouble finding at least several that can offer this to you.

Put together a flyer announcing a free one-hour informational seminar which will be about whatever particular area of your industry you wish to discuss. Use the chapter on free email newsletters for ideas. It shouldn't be too difficult to come up with at least several possibilities. Get enough flyers out in the immediate surrounding area and require that anyone who wishes to attend must R.S.V.P. because space is limited.

(Arrange things so that space IS limited. Base it on how many people you're comfortable talking to and how much you're willing to budget on this.)

It's best to offer perhaps two menu items as options and to pre-arrange this with the restaurant. Make sure this is something the restaurant will allow. You don't want ten people coming in all ordering filet mignon and lobster when you assumed they'd all get the burger when you planned your budget for this event.

Show up at least fifteen or twenty minutes before the scheduled start time. You want to let the restaurant manager know you're there, make sure your wishes for menu options are all set, and make sure your designated area is in order. If you're using a flipchart or whiteboard or some other display device, get it set up now before any of your prospects arrive.

Now it's showtime. Take a few moments to introduce yourself to each prospect and chat for a few minutes. While I don't believe in dwelling on "rapport building" in a sales appointment, it's extremely important here. You're in a casual setting, your prospects will be at ease and generally in a good mood (after all, they're getting a free lunch out of the deal) and open and receptive to you and what you have to say. After introductions and ordering, get up there and talk about whatever you're going to talk about. Keep it informal. If it's a small group, you may even prefer to sit with them during lunch and talk from there, which is an especially good way to keep the atmosphere light.

Towards the end of your informational session, remind everyone of what you do, what you sell, and, most importantly, how they can benefit. Chances are at least one or two people will approach you on their own and express an interest in at least considering a purchase from you. Regardless of how many approach you, it's important to exchange cards with everyone there, and it's best to do this as they arrive so you don't miss anyone on the way out.

Later that day, email a thank-you note to each attendee. If you happened to get any cards without an email address, mail a thank-you note. Let them know you're available to serve their needs. About a week later, you should call to arrange an appointment. (This is another exception to my hard-and-fast rules. Because you've already met these people and communicated on a personal level, it's better for you to call yourself, rather than have your appointment setter do it.)

Like I said, start small. Build up to bigger and better things. I know of some financial services salespeople who hold very large evening seminars with a hundred or more people in attendance. This obviously requires quite a bit more advance planning and a larger budget, but why not aspire to do it as well? Faithfully carry out the strategies presented in this program and you'll be there sooner than you think.

## Little or no Cost – Teleseminars

Teleseminars are extremely popular in my line of work. And why not? They enable authors such as myself to do the following, at almost no cost, and frequently for free when using a free teleconferencing service:

- Teleseminars allow me to provide value and useful information to prospects at no cost to them.

- Teleseminars are a form of free publicity.

- Teleseminars position me as the authority figure because I'm the speaker and the listeners are my audience.

- Teleseminars are just as effective, and in many ways *more effective* than a regular free seminar, and at far less cost.

How are teleseminars more effective than the free seminars I've just convinced you are so effective? Simple. It's that one word I've already taught you, that one word that can spell the difference between making a good income and getting rich. That word, of course, is **leverage**.

A free seminar is limited by space, cost, and other factors. A teleseminar can be unlimited. *I conduct them from the convenience of my own home and frequently have thousands of people listening in at once!* THAT is leverage!

Teleseminars are also great because you can use them with your existing list. Your newsletter list. And you'd better work on building a newsletter list if you want to be a top producer. Teleseminars leverage your list by getting them proactive rather than just reactive by reading your e-mails and hopefully responding to you.

And, of course, you don't need to restrict teleseminars to your newsletter list. You want to constantly *add* prospects to your pipeline, and you do that by using my other techniques such as mass flyer distribution. Now go get on the web, find a free or cheap teleconference service, and get to work scheduling your first teleseminar! I promise the sales you'll get from it will be well worth your time and will be more than you can get from months of cold calling!

## Free and Easy Publicity on the Web

One of my favorite tools on the Internet is the use of free press release services. My favorite is PRWeb.com. I won't go into too much detail here – the site is pretty self-explanatory – but I will say that the use of these services has brought both myself and my clients a TON of business we would have never found otherwise. They are also very, very effective in lending credibility to yourself. You can print your press releases (PRWeb.com will provide you with a printable .pdf version of yours) and include it with proposals, in your email newsletters, or as part of the media kit you will use to get more media coverage. Reporters love press releases. In the media world, they equal credibility!

In order to get an idea of how to craft your press release, go to PRWeb.com and run a search under my name. You can read releases I've issued in the past, and get a good feel for how I took my product (this book) and made it newsworthy. Then you can think of how you will make your product newsworthy so that reporters and prospects will contacts you via your press release.

It's important to have your website up and running before doing releases. People who wouldn't call *will* click through to your website (included in the contact info section of the release) and either contact you then, or get on your free newsletter list so you can permanently have them in your pipeline. Either way, press releases are a fantastic tool that salespeople almost never use, so take advantage!

## Using Seminars – Action Items

- Seminars are a great way to neutralize the minds of your prospective customers and to allow them to see you as an impartial expert instead of a salesperson.

- If you have a fear or disdain of public speaking, immediately begin taking steps to overcome it. Join Toastmasters or take a public speaking course. This will not only condition you for public speaking but will also improve your communication skills on all levels.

- Start small. Plan a small luncheon for ten or less attendees. If nothing else, look at it as practice for future seminars.

- Build up to larger and larger events. Your reputation and level of respect will rapidly build. You will be seen as an expert in your field of endeavor rather than a salesperson.

- Teleseminars are cheaper and easier to set up than regular free seminars, and incorporate the magical power of leverage. Get started right now on setting up your first free teleseminar.

- Get instant credibility and media coverage through the use of free or low-cost press releases from outlets such as PRWeb.com.

# Speak to Sell

*"I'm not particularly tall, but when I'm up on a seminar stage, I'm towering over everyone on the room."*

*-Frank Rumbauskas*

One of the most overlooked, but most effective, methods of getting hot prospects approaching you while also building your expert status in your community is to do free speaking to prospect-rich audiences. This method is especially easy because the organizations you'll speak to are always hungry for new, interesting speakers for their meetings.

Before beginning, you'll need to decide on a topic, and create your presentation. It needs to be something that will catch a business owner's interest, without necessarily giving away what it is that you do.

For example, my free speaking topic is "The Largest Hidden Expense in Business." I then present on how extremely expensive sales turnover is, and go on to explain that cold calling is the single largest cause of turnover among salespeople, and I back up my statements with evidence and statistics. This results in business owners and sales directors asking me to come out and teach their own sales teams my strategies, for a fee of course.

If I had named my presentation "Never Cold Call Again" or "How to Sell Without Cold Calling," people would write it off as just another sales presentation and not show up. But talking about the largest hidden cost in every business gets them interested, and they show up.

A friend of a friend is an asset protection attorney, who uses this strategy to show people how easily an enemy armed with a predatory lawyer can take their assets. He signs at least two new clients at each presentation for fees averaging over ten thousand dollars each.

You don't have to be in B2B sales to make this work. Business owners are real people who also happen to be consumers, so if you're in B2C, you can easily come up with a presentation and a catchy title.

## Your Presentation

Presentations should be slide-driven, whether you choose to use PowerPoint or Excel. Keep it on your laptop and ready to go. If they're providing a computer, put it on a flash drive and bring it with you. Also, find out what kind of computer and what version of software they use. If you're using Apple Keynote, for example, and they have a Windows PC, you'll need to export to the appropriate version of PowerPoint.

Most groups also have a projector, so have the correct adapter cable for your laptop to plug into a projector, and have a remote so you can forward through the slides.

Never, ever read directly from your slides. To be totally honest, I use slides as my own outline so I don't have to look down at notes throughout a presentation.

Most importantly, in writing your presentation, you MUST NOT sell! Selling directly to the audience is a sure way to never be invited to speak again. What you need to do is create interest and desire, while establishing your own credibility. Present problems, and how they can be solved - like how eliminating cold calling will also eliminate that huge hidden cost in business. As always, be creative and brainstorm as much as you can.

## Finding Speaking Opportunities

This is the easy part! Here is a partial list of who to contact for free speaking opportunities:

- Rotary Clubs. This is the most plentiful, and easiest opportunity to get. Furthermore, Rotary Clubs are frequented by desirable prospects such as business owners, attorneys, accountants, and more. Many influential people are members and it's a fantastic opportunity to establish your own expert status while finding new referral partners.

- Chambers of Commerce. Chambers are another opportunity. I don't like them as much as Rotary because you'll frequently be presenting to other salespeople, rather than influential members of the community, but there will always be plenty of small business owners in attendance.

- Alumni clubs. This one is overlooked, but is a great source of leads. I stumbled on this one when a neighbor who went to Harvard Business School invited me to come speak at their monthly breakfast meeting. Granted, I was in front of a room full of Harvard MBAs so they were all very successful businesspeople, but I've found that alumni clubs in general, and business school alumni clubs in particular, are fantastic places to speak.

- Private executive groups. These are the toughest to get into, but the best lead source once you're in. Renaissance Executive Clubs is just one example of an organization where the audience is almost entirely C-Level executives, and who are looking for regular speakers for their meetings.

- Mothers of Preschoolers (MOPS): I'm adding this to get those of you in B2C sales to start thinking outside the box. Mothers are prime prospects for a *ton* of products, far beyond the usual suspects like insurance and real estate. Brainstorm and you'll come up with other great venues: PTA meetings for moms, golf clubs and cigar clubs to reach dads and affluent consumers, and so on.


When speaking to these groups, I recommend sticking around for the duration of the meeting, and even show up early so you can meet and greet everyone as they arrive.

This is also a good time to consider writing your own book and having it printed. Writing a book isn't hard: If you're already writing valuable articles and email newsletters, you can simply compile that content into a book. That's how my friend and fellow author Jeffrey Gitomer got started.

A neighbor of mine is an expert on business etiquette, who enjoys a large following and speaks for hefty fees. She has done just that: Written her own book and had it handsomely printed. She hands them out at speaking events like the one I've explained in this chapter, and it carries a lot more weight than giving out just another business card!

**BONUS**: These speaking opportunities are not only wonderful for generating interest and leads among highly desirable prospects, but they're also rich with highly desirable referral partners, so get to know people and keep in touch. Get business cards and offer to take people to lunch. You'll be surprised at the lucrative relationships, and even genuine friendships, that will follow.

**HINT**: If you don't think you're a very good speaker, or have too much stage fright to begin this strategy, join Toastmasters. It's a great place to start, and quickly develop skill as a powerful speaker. Just be forwarded that some Toastmasters clubs are full of people trying to sign you up for their latest MLM or business opportunity so you may have to try a few out before finding your group.

### Speak to Sell – Action Items

- Come up with a title for your presentation, one that will catch the interest of business owners or other important prospects. Keep the "How to Succeed in Sales" guidelines in mind.

- Develop and practice your presentation. Create an attractive PowerPoint to go with it, or pay someone to have it done professionally.

- If you're not comfortable with public speaking, join Toastmasters or sign up for a public speaking class.

- Contact local, prospect-rich groups such as Rotary Clubs, Chambers of Commerce, Alumni Clubs, and paid executive organizations, and offer to speak for free.

- Show up early and stay late in order to network and exchange business cards with your audience.

- Never directly sell in your presentations; instead, provide valuable, interesting content of use to your audience.

- Follow up with these people. They are prime prospects because, by speaking, you have created a power paradigm wherein you are seen by them as a leader, an expert, and a person of power. All of these factors will make them more pre-disposed to buy from you.

# Gain Instant Credibility Over Your Competitors

*"Remember, perception is everything. Whatever prospects perceive you to be is what they will believe you to be. So create the perception of massive credibility, and your competition will be shut out."*

*-Frank Rumbauskas*

As I've covered extensively, one of the biggest problems with cold calling is that it destroys your status as a business equal, authority figure, and expert. Since not being seen as the expert authority figure is disastrous to sales success, doesn't it make sense that being seen as the expert will send your sales through the roof?

Well, guess what – there's a quick and easy way to become the expert. For real. Confirmed by a third party and everything.

You now know that a free, informational newsletter will not only maintain constant, ongoing contact with your prospects – especially when automated through the use of an autoresponder system such as aweber.com – but it also gives you tons of credibility that your competitors don't have because it makes you a knowledgeable expert, in writing. However, you can take that a step further, in fact a lot of steps further, by using the simple strategy I'm about to reveal to you.

On the web, there are tons of free reprint articles. They are exactly as their name implies: articles available for free reprint anywhere and everywhere, and we've already seen in the chapter on newsletters how you don't even need to write your own newsletter – you can simply fill it with free reprint articles and slap your name and phone number on it. By actually writing free reprint articles, though, you become an expert. Here's how:

There are plenty of free reprint article sites. My personal favorite is ezinearticles.com. You can write an article and submit it to ezinearticles.com, right now, for free (many sites charge to list your articles). Now here's the best part: Once you've submitted a few articles to their site, they will list them all on one page, complete with your name as the 'Expert Author.' You can print one or all of the articles, or you can take the URL that links to your Expert Author page and distribute it freely. You know, to prospects and everyone on your newsletter list. Heck, why not add 'Expert Author' to your business cards and flyers and include the link there?

As you can imagine, this one trick will blow your competition out of the water! Think about how close so many sales are … how your price was 2% higher than the competitor's, but your product and service were the same and you had no way of finding any more value to bring to the prospect. But, if you could differentiate yourself by showing that prospect a third-party website officially certifying you as the Expert, don't you think that prospect would immediately want to trust you more than the nearest competitor? Or all of your competitors for that matter?

Writing a few good articles, contributing them, then including your Expert Author page in places where prospects will find it (like your business cards, your flyers, your sales letters, any direct mail pieces you do, in your newsletters, and especially on your website), will do so much for your credibility, you have no idea until you actually do it. So get writing! Keep articles to around 500 words. That way the prospects won't be scared off by something too long and will actually read them. Also, it's best to put the link to your Expert Author page where prospects will 'find' it rather than overtly showing it to them. It's like buying a new Mercedes, then telling everyone, "Hey, look at me, I drive a Mercedes." The accomplished people in this world don't do that … they simply keep their mouths shut and let their status symbols speak for themselves. The same is true for your articles. A true expert doesn't need to say, "Hey, look at me, I'm the expert." True experts let that speak for themselves.

Another really awesome way to become a recognized expert is through the use of free e-books. Creating an e-book is quite simple. You type up the document in Word, then convert it to a .pdf file. (Don't have .pdf creation software? It's built into Macs, and if you're on a Windows computer, there are plenty of free .pdf software programs available on the web for download.)

An excellent example of a free e-book that is designed to drive sales is one you may very well have already – the free e-book I give away at www.nevercoldcall.com. In fact, it's merely a compilation of several free reprint articles I did quite a while ago, so it didn't take any writing to put it together. See, if you've done your free reprint articles, you probably have enough content for a free e-book! I simply organized my free reprint articles into chapters, added a table of contents, and saved it to a .pdf file. You probably noticed I did something else – I included links to sign up for my free newsletter and to a tell-a-friend form. Tell-a-friend forms are great. Do a search online for them, you'll find tons of free information on how to set one up at no cost just like I did.

Think of how much credibility you have when contacting a prospect for the very first time. Let's say you normally e-mail prospects with an introductory e-mail, stating who you are and inviting the prospect to sign up for your free newsletter at your site. How much more professional and credible will you sound when you email introducing yourself as an author and either attaching your e-book, or providing the prospect a link where it can be downloaded and read for free?

Combine this with the Expert Author page you now know about, and you have a serious one-two punch that raises your credibility and authority so many levels above your competition's that they won't even stand a chance against you!

# Be a Consultant, not a "Consultative Salesperson"

*One of the central concepts of the Never Cold Call Again philosophy is that of giving value before expecting to receive anything in return. You saw how this is done with free seminars, free newsletters, and more.*

*Now you'll learn how to apply this concept when you're face-to-face with prospects.*

The term "consultative selling" is running rampant these days.

It's a big lie.

It insults the prospect's intelligence.

Salespeople who buy into the idea of "consultative selling" and who expect prospects to buy into it are only fooling themselves. They're deceiving nobody but themselves.

Furthermore, this concept of "consultative selling" is extremely offensive to true consultants, who are experts in their respective fields and who offer truly helpful, unbiased advice to their clients.

Never tell a prospect that your job is to recommend a solution through a consultative process. Never, ever say that you and your company wish to "partner" with them. Partner relationships and vendor-customer relationships aren't even remotely similar. If you and your customer were true business partners, it would be in your best interests to provide them with your product or service for free, or at the very least, below cost. In the real world we operate in, that's obviously NOT in your best interests, or even remotely possible for that matter.

However, there is a way around all of this. Instead of lying to your prospects by claiming to be a "consultative salesperson" or someone who wishes to "partner" with them, become a consultant or find ways to help them in ways that a true partner would. For real.

This isn't as difficult as it may sound. I did it in the telecom world. Although my goal was to get the customer to buy my Internet access or phone system, I offered them free services as part of my sales process. Now and again when I was meeting with a customer regarding a telephone system or telecom services they'd said something like "Oh darn, by the way, we need to move the fax line to the front office. It's really inconvenient to have to walk back here all the time to send a fax. How much will that cost?" Guess what I did? Wrote up an order to have a technician come out, move the fax line, and bill them $250 for a visit charge plus one hour of labor? Hell no. I went out to my car, grabbed my telephone lineman's tools that I happened to keep in there, and took care of it at no charge. If the customer asked me what they owed or what the charge is, I'd say "Don't worry about it, no big deal." If they asked if I used to be a technician or how I learned those skills, I'd embellish a bit and tell them the company teaches us that as part of training in order to make sure we, as salespeople, can provide the highest level of service and guarantee that we wouldn't screw up any orders due to lack of knowledge in that area.

What did all my competition do when the customer mentioned moving a fax line or whatever else they happened to need? You guessed it. They called out a technician, which cost the customer a pretty penny, or added the same cost as a line item into their proposal. Guess who got the business? You guessed right again. I did.

The underlying principle here goes back to a basic truth that can be found explained in Ralph Waldo Emerson's essay on Compensation. If you haven't read it, do so immediately. Buy yourself a copy or find it online and print it. Read it no less than a hundred times. Every time you read it you will discover new truths. The bottom line is this: You must give before you can expect to receive. The free services in the capacity of a consultant, the free informational email newsletter you're sending out, and the free informational seminars you're going to do are all examples of the Law of Compensation at work. That's why it's so important to focus on these activities on things that truly do benefit the customer rather than an obvious attempt to sell them something. It's well worth the payoff. Read "Grow Rich Through Peace Of Mind" by Napoleon Hill. An entire chapter of that book is dedicated to a discussion of Emerson's Law of Compensation, and the story of how Dr. Hill came to meet his wife is a grand example of the Law in action.

Robert T. Kiyosaki, in one of his "Rich Dad, Poor Dad" audio programs I listened to recently, explained it in a different way, a way that is more relevant to our purposes here. He explains that the Industrial Age was all about greed and hoarding, while the Information Age, by sharp contrast, is all about generosity and giving. He goes on to explain that his great success with the "Rich Dad, Poor Dad" website has a lot to do with the fact that the site's purpose is to freely share information and give away information and advice that, in the old Industrial Age way of doing things, would never have been offered for free.

So, how do you go about becoming a consultant, offering free help and advice to your prospects and customers? It's easy. Find something related to your particular product that customers normally have to pay for. You'll probably have to be creative. For me, it was the example I mentioned, plus many others as well. I offered free assistance to customers with their phone systems, computer networks, Internet access, and anything else I could think of, even when those products were supplied by someone other than me. In other words, my competition. Customers were used to paying at least $100/hour for computer network and phone system help. Perhaps they paid $25/call to a hotline for questions on programming their phones, or cleaning up some mess they accidentally caused in their computers. By offering free help with these issues, I accomplished what so many of the other techniques in this book accomplish: I forever locked up those prospects for myself, shutting out the competition before they ever got one foot in the door.

Acting as a free, professional consultant will have other effects you otherwise would've never even imagined. Prospects and customers will come to respect and even depend upon your advice and opinions. Some will view you as a valued resource. The financial benefit to you, in this type of situation, will be the tremendous amount of referral business that will come your way. More than any other type of lead, these referrals will already be your customers *before* you even meet them. The power behind that kind of referral is unbeatable, and, once again, your competition will never have any chance of selling those prospects, EVER.

## Be a Consultant, not a "Consultative Salesperson"
### Action Items

- Find ways that you can provide useful, free services to your prospects without any expectation of anything in return.

- Do not accept offers of payment or compensation for these services. Refusing to do so will set the eternal Law of Compensation to work for you.

- Prospects who don't even buy from you, for whatever reason, will send you quality referrals as a form of compensation for your services.

- Provide the referrals you receive from these people with the same level of service and respect.

- You will become a trusted, respected, and even depended-upon advisor to the people you serve.

- Your power of leverage now increases in a dimension quite different from that of mere numbers. You gain an influence over prospects, customers, and their colleagues that can be gained in no other way and that can be matched in no other way.

# Networking that WORKS

*"Money talks, B.S. walks."*

*- Basic truth*

I wasted more time than you can possibly imagine pursuing fruitless attempts at networking.

Perhaps you have too.

I'm sure you know EXACTLY what I'm talking about.

Since I'm not even close to being a morning person to begin with, I wasn't particularly amused with getting up at an obscene hour to attend a 7am 'leads club' meeting (that I had to pay for, by the way), only to sit there with a bunch of other bleary-eyed, unable-to-function-that-early-in-the-morning salespeople who brought nothing to the table. Literally nothing. Just a knee-jerk "I don't have any leads this week."

After ruining several otherwise good days by getting up way too early, I found some happy hour 'leads clubs.' I had a great time drinking and shooting pool with everyone else who showed up, but that's all it turned out to be – drinking and shooting pool. In all fairness, they should really drop the 'leads club' from the name and simply call it happy hour because that's all it turned out to be.

Next, I started attending chamber of commerce mixers. Don't even get me started on this one. These were so useless it was almost embarrassing. To make matters worse, the week following any chamber event was spent dodging salespeople who happened to get one of my cards and who were trying to call and sell ME something. I can't tell you how many times I had these guys call my office phone, then my cell phone, then my office phone, then finally leave a message and send an email a minute later. Most were life insurance salesmen who obviously weren't aware of the fact that I was single with no dependents. Perhaps I should have that fact printed on my cards from now on.

Next, I sought out more "exclusive" and "professional" networking organizations. I found one in particular that claimed to be very, very "exclusive" and in fact operated like a private club. You were allowed to attend one or two events by invitation only, because they were, of course, closed to "outsiders." After doing so, you could apply for membership, but only if your application was endorsed by two "sponsors" who were limited to members in good standing. Then you had to endure a telephone interview with two different "board members." Wow, I thought, this must really be worth something. If I can just get into this group I'll have found the pot of gold and all the powerful connections I'll ever need!

I sought out my invitation to their next event and got it. I showed up dressed in my best $3,000 Oxxford Clothes suit, feeling, as Napoleon Hill described in his story in Chapter 9, "as rich as Rockefeller."

The group appeared to be the same people from the chamber of commerce. In fact, one insurance salesman in particular who drove me absolutely insane with incessant sales calls, was there collecting as many cards as he possibly could.

For the evening's "featured speaker," a couple of run-of-the-mill web designers hooked their laptop up to the projector, showed some web pages they had done, and that was it. I thought to myself, "you've got to be kidding me," and started trying to come up creative ways to dodge the weeks' worth of calls I was about to endure from that pushy insurance salesmen I had mentioned.

It became painfully clear to me that the purpose of this group was to create a "private club" and a feeling of "exclusivity" for a bunch of people who had neither the means nor the social graces to join a REAL private social club such as the Arizona Club or University Club that we have here in Phoenix.  I was angry that not only my time was wasted, but that I had been duped into believing that I had finally found the holy grail of networking groups.

After all that, I found a very novel concept that causes otherwise useless people to suddenly come up with quite a few leads and unhesitatingly hand them over to you.

It's based on the undisputed truth of life that "money talks and b.s. walks."

Tell someone you'll give them money for a lead and they suddenly come up with a bunch of real, qualified leads.

Most companies have some sort of referral program in place.  If not, offer a piece of your after-tax commissions.  Giving up 25% of your commission on a sale is a tiny price to pay for a sale that you otherwise would've never gotten in the first place.  What's more, most of them are pre-qualified and open to meeting with you.  I've shared this idea with salespeople I've both worked with and coached.  I love sending them out to put it to work, then two weeks later when they're schedule is packed with appointments they get all bright-eyed and say, "wow, tell people you'll give them money for sales and the leads come pouring in!"

If your company doesn't have a referral program, talk to your manager about it.  In more than one instance I did this and a short time later it was in place.  One even built it into the sale – if I was offering a $100 referral fee for leads to my networking partners, we buried $100 into the proposal in the labor costs or some other soft cost.

The best part about all this is that you can have several competing salespeople signed up and all giving you leads because you never have to reciprocate.  They're getting paid.  You owe them no leads in return.  When I was selling phone systems, I had no less than five competitive local telephone companies on my "payroll," as I liked to call it, and there were no issues whatsoever.  I kept all information confidential.  When a lead came to me, it stopped there, and I shared the information with no one.  It was safe for those salespeople to give me the names of people they were working with even though they knew full well that I had the same arrangement with most or all of their competitors.

This can work anywhere, even at the dreaded chamber of commerce.  Show up, tell people what you do, then tell them you'll give them money for leads that turn into sales.  As if by a stroke of magic, those people who said "great, I'll keep that in mind" suddenly can think of half a dozen people who might need to talk to you.

## Business Networking Websites

A recent development that is getting great results for lots and lots of salespeople, myself included, are the business networking sites that have popped up over the last year or two and gained millions of members.  The best of these, by far, is LinkedIn.com. Buy one of their premium memberships that will give you the ability to contact people directly, without the need to be connected first.

On these sites you fill out a thorough personal profile that is searchable by others.  You can also search for people you know in order to add yourself to their networks.  This is key – on some of the sites, for example LinkedIn.com, you cannot contact another person unless you have an 'introduction' from someone whose network you are already a part of. So, it's important to get yourself into as many networks as possible. Once you do, the site has a viral effect in that your name spreads to more and more other people's networks. For example, let's say you're in John Doe's network. He has twenty people in his network, who each have twenty people in theirs, who each have ten people in theirs, and so on. By being linked in to all those people, indirectly through several layers of contact, you have the ability to connect to those people that you otherwise wouldn't if you were not in the first level network.

I've met some very high-level people through these sites, such as authors and CEOs, so it's well worth your time to check them out and get profiles built on them. You'll be glad you did, and it's fantastic that the Information Age and the Internet are replacing the old-school, worthless leads clubs and chamber mixers with something that really works!

## Networking that WORKS – Action Items

- **Networking is a good concept in theory but rarely produces big results in the real world**

- **Networking events, chamber mixers, and the like usually have the end result of salespeople chasing YOU instead of providing leads**

- **Most 'leads clubs' are worthless. Some are nothing more than a scam to collect membership fees. If you're considering one, be sure to hear some testimonials from existing members, and be certain those members aren't getting a referral fee to get you to sign up**

- **People who are otherwise poor sources of leads can magically think of many when you offer them money**

- **Napoleon Hill said: 'No intelligent person will work for you without adequate compensation." Therefore, don't insult the intelligence of others by simply asking for leads and referrals. Offer them adequate compensation in return.**

- **Your power of leverage explodes as those on your "payroll" spread the word to others and suddenly you have dozens of people sending you good, qualified, ready-to-buy referrals**

# Use Publicity – It's Free Advertising

*"Use the power of legitimacy.  What is seen in
print is never questioned."*

*- Herb Cohen*

We salespeople aren't the only ones out there prospecting, searching for new leads and seeking new business.

There's another group of professionals who do this in an almost daily basis.

Journalists.

Reporters.

Say what?  Journalists spend time prospecting?

That's right.  And like us, there's nothing they love more than a call-in.  So give them one.

Salespeople almost universally fail to use the power of free publicity that most of them have readily available at their fingertips.  The misconception out there is that getting yourself written up in a local newspaper or magazine is extremely difficult and reserved only for those of noteworthy accomplishments.

Not true.

Like so many other half-truths, this one also does more harm than a blatant falsehood.

The fact is that somewhere in your community, a reporter for a local publication is looking for something new to write about and YOU would be perfect.

Think I'm kidding?

Take a look at your city or town's local "Business Journal."  There is a standard publication called the "Business Journal" currently in publication in 55 markets.  (For a list, see their website at www.bizjournals.com.)

In addition, nearly every city and town has one or more local or neighborhood papers separate from the one or two major newspapers in that market.  For example, back in the Phoenix area, where I used to live, in addition to the major newspaper we have the East Valley Tribune, Scottsdale Tribune, West Valley Tribune, North Scottsdale Times, and half a dozen others.  I once had my color photo dead center on the front page of the Scottsdale Tribune without having to try very hard.  At the time I was nothing more than a lowly Internet access salesman.  Ask for the moon and chances are you'll get it.  That may be a cliché, but in this case it's usually true.

Gather up the local papers and Business Journal for your area (if you have only one paper without any independents, chances are you're in a smaller market and can realistically get into that paper).  Read through them, spot the articles related to your industry, and note the journalist's name and contact information if it happens to be listed.  Nowadays, nearly all publications include the reporter's email address at the end of the article. (Hmm, I wonder if he or she can benefit from your free informational newsletter?)

In many cases a polite phone call or email to the appropriate reporter will do.  Offer to take them lunch for the opportunity to meet with them.  Even though these people must actively prospect for good topics to write about, the key word here is good.  They get tons of calls and emails from hucksters and scam artists who are looking for free advertising or to get their 'fifteen minutes of fame' but who have nothing of interest to offer. Chances are, you'll have to ignite your flames of creativity once again and come up with an angle.

There are a few ways to go here. You can be the impartial, professional consultant, talking about a topic of interest in your field of expertise, providing information that will be beneficial and useful to those who read the article (keep the Law of Compensation always in mind). Or you can talk about our product or service itself, provided that you talk about how it is very unique or is helping to benefit people or businesses in a great way. Although this is really is free advertising, the reporter's purpose isn't to run a free ad for you. Their purpose is to have an interesting story that is of interest but also impartial. They have a reputation to uphold and nothing will destroy it faster than publishing articles that shamelessly promote a commercial product or service.

If you think that getting an article written about you in a local newspaper is difficult, think again. The Phoenix Business Journal serves all of the Phoenix metropolitan area, nearly four million people. For the cost of a few inexpensive lunches, we pulled it off three times in a six month period. That's right, three times in six months. And we were nothing more than an Internet service provider, not the inventors of some space-age new product that was a magnet for media attention. If you build a good relationship with your new journalist friend from the start, getting subsequent articles published is a piece of cake. In fact, as was our experience, they'll call YOU and ask YOU for YOUR permission to publish another article about YOU in issues where they're drawing a blank or can't find anything worthwhile to write about. That first one was the most difficult for us. From then on, a nice lunch now and then kept the program on autopilot.

The other option aside from making personal contact with a reporter is to issue a press release. This is a piece of cake and nearly any local paper or other local business publication will run it. In fact, it will probably show up on websites and prospects searching for information on what you do will stumble upon it online, thereby generating more leads for you.

Even if it's nothing more than a simple product announcement or statement of what you do, if it's written properly it will usually work.

Because formats for press releases vary greatly and the content will largely depend on your product or service and how it's different, we won't go into the details of how to write press releases here. Our job is to let you know that it's readily available to you, is far, far easier than you probably thought, and will yield amazing results. Search online for information, or check out some books on public relations. They'll tell you everything you need to know in glorious detail.

Alternately, you can hire a public relations expert or firm to do your press release but this may be cost-prohibitive

(IMPORTANT NOTE: Never put any time or effort into what this chapter discusses until you've gotten your website online. That web address is critical to have in any and all of your prospecting and marketing efforts. Be sure to never leave it absent from ANYTHING!)

Almost NO salespeople do these things. DO them and shut out your competition!

## Use Publicity:  It's Free Advertising – Action Items

- Gather up copies of as many local newspapers and business publications as you can find, most importantly your city's Business Journal if you're in one of their 55 markets

- Find articles relevant to your industry and record the names and contact information of the reporters who cover your industry

- A polite call or email to these reporters, preferably with an offer to meet for lunch, will almost always get you in front of the right ones

- Build a good relationship with your new reporter friend.  Doing so will guarantee subsequent follow-up articles after your first one is published

- Educate yourself on writing press releases through many of the books written on the subject or with information you uncover online

- Write and properly issue a good, solid, concise press release

- The power of legitimacy and perception are now working in your favor. Being in mainstream print automatically gives you LEGITIMACY.  You are now perceived as an EXPERT, a LEADER in your field, a person of POWER, and possibly even FAME.  This has untold effects on your now awesome power of leverage.

# A System of Systems – Making it all Flow

*"Do it now!"*

*- W. Clement Stone*

I get lots of feedback from salespeople claiming that my techniques are too simplistic, and won't work for 'their' products and services.    What lots of salespeople who say that aren't remembering is that your ultimate goal should not be to use these techniques at random, but instead to integrate them into a master system of systems that will generate more hot, qualified, ready-to-buy leads than you know what to do with.

Here's an example.  One of the biggest objections I get is similar to the following:

*"Flyer distribution?   You've got to be kidding me.   That's for selling junk and commodity products.   Crap everyone is selling and nobody is interested in.   I'm a big man selling big stuff – that's not good enough for me.   Give me some real sales techniques that I can use, not this beginner crap."*

Well ... I have to laugh when I hear that one.  I laugh because of how many big-ticket sales I made that started out with a flyer, and how many people I know who are earning six-figures in commissions thanks to flyer distribution.  But ... the catch is that flyers aren't the end-all, be-all. They simply start the process.

**They are step #1 in the System of Systems.**

(Remember, this is an example.  Flyers may or may not be the ideal first step in your individual system of systems.  My goal here is just to get you thinking in terms of big systems rather than a series of unrelated individual techniques.)

About a week ago I had the pleasure of being the guest on a Simpleology Live Learning Event conducted by #1 best-selling author Mark Joyner.  Someone had faxed a question for me into Mark's office prior to the call.   The question was, simply, how could a technique like flyer distribution ever work for big-ticket items?  Aren't flyers for low-price commodity items like cell phones and car insurance?

Nope.

Here's the explanation I gave during the teleseminar:

In big-ticket sales (I think this person sold very high-end management consulting services), the key is to have your entire self-marketing infrastructure in place *before* you start sending your flyers out to speak for you.  By infrastructure, I mean essentials such as:

- Your personal website (a must-have ... no exceptions)

- Your newsletter and autoresponder series (several newsletters should be pre-written and already saved into your autoresponder account before you begin marketing yourself)
- A sign-up form on your website for your free newsletter/autoresponder
- Several well-written articles, preferably on an 'Expert Author' page as previously discussed.

Once you have those essentials in place, it's time to craft your flyer.  As you now know, effective flyers typically end in your contact information and a fax-back form.

**In this case, and for high-ticket sales in general, your flyer should be crafted with the goal of sending readers to your website to sign up for your free newsletter.  That's it.  Products requiring long sales cycles naturally work better with a longer self-marketing cycle.**

You of course want to include your name and telephone number on the flyer, but your goal here isn't to get a call.  It's great if you do but it makes more sense to get them to your website and onto your newsletter list.  When writing the flyer text and headline(s), remember that your goal is to get them to subscribe to your newsletter.  So, with that in mind, make it enticing.  Give them something they want.  If you're selling life insurance, don't say, "Sign up for my free monthly newsletter chock full of great information about insurance."  Nope.  Give them something they *really* want.  Like this: "Sign up for my free monthly newsletter, full of tips on how to reduce your taxes legally and how to make your investments work harder for you now so you won't have to work hard later."  THAT is want people want!

Remember, a big part of buying is emotional, so speak to their emotions.  This applies equally in business-to-business sales as in business-to-consumer.

Again, flyers are an example.  You might start out with a postcard mailing that directs people to a website and newsletter signup.  Or you may send out a well-written letter that invites prospects to a free seminar.  Or perhaps an email blast to your existing newsletter list that invites prospects to listen to a free teleseminar. The possibilities are endless.

DO THIS RIGHT NOW:  Take a look at all of the techniques presented in this book, think about them, and think about all the different combinations you can put together in building your system of systems.  Remember, a one-two punch hits twice as hard as one lone punch, so don't squander these ideas by using them alone and at random.  They'll still work, but will work only half as well as if you put them together in some deadly one-two or even one-two-three combinations. Do it now!

# Part 4: The *Never Cold Call Again*® Social Media Selling System

# Everything You Know About Social Media Is Wrong!

If there's one catchphrase I've come to really hate in recent years, it's "social media."

Or, I should say, I used to hate it. Once I learned how to use it, I finally warmed up to it. But to be honest, I still seriously hate the way people are using it, and, more to the point, how many hucksters are out there selling books and courses on social media that are totally worthless.

The truth of the matter is that most people are making money with social media by, well, teaching others how to make money with social media. Very few are using it effectively, because no one has ever taught them how.

So going into this section of the course, I will ask you to keep an open mind. If you've also found just about every social media course to be rubbish, as I have, it's time for you to start over with a clean slate.

The major problem with the use - or should I say, the misuse - of social media is that no one is doing it in an organized and effective way. Most social media "strategies" consist of one or more of the following:

 - Posting random tweets on Twitter and hoping they'll stick

 - Using "auto follow" software to accumulate thousands of Twitter followers and Facebook fans, who will never buy anything

 - Set up a Facebook page and wonder why nothing happens

 - Put up a LinkedIn profile and wonder why nothing happens

... and so on.

The Never Cold Call Again social media strategy, however, is organized. It is based on the concept of first, creating content that is not only useful to prospective customers, and second, using social media in an automated and organized manner to propagate that content all over the Internet.

Here's how it all works:

1. Your blog is the hub of it all. I'm going to show you how to set up a free WordPress blog, and then optimize is so the search engines will LOVE it.

2. Your blog will automatically feed to your Twitter account, and tweet every new post and piece of content you create.

3. Twitter will automatically feed to Facebook and LinkedIn and auto post each new tweet on those pages.

4. You'll then take each blog post, and create a video to post on YouTube.

5. You'll export the audio portion of the video, and upload it as an iTunes podcast. You'll also upload the video portion to iTunes as a video podcast.

6. You'll create a PowerPoint presentation laying out the major points of each blog post, and upload it to multiple presentation sites.

7. You'll do a voiceover on the PowerPoint to create another video for YouTube and iTunes.

8. You'll create a PDF version of each post, to upload to various document websites.

9. Convert your blog posts to press releases - either free or paid - to bring you expert status and leads.

As you can see, this is very comprehensive. In addition, it's VERY easy to create a HUGE amount of content from just one little blog post than only takes you five or ten minutes to write!

Typical social media "strategy" completely misses the most important thing about social media: Content is king! Content is what people love. Having thousands of Twitter followers or Facebook fans is utterly useless if you're not flooding them with high-quality content, that will get people to first find you, second to buy from you, and third to get them spreading the word about you.

I'm going to show you even more great ways to attract new business, on top of all of the above, so let's get started!

**DISCLAIMER**: This section of the course will have you setting up shop on a lot of social media web properties: Facebook, Twitter, LinkedIn, WordPress, iTunes, just to name a few. Giving specific, detailed instructions on how to register and get set up on each property is beyond the scope of this course, for the reason that most are self-explanatory and if help is needed it's readily available online, for free, and also because they change so frequently that putting such information into this book may make it obsolete before the ink is even dry.

For that reason, I'll show you exactly how you're going to employ each social media property, and why, but will skip the basics of how to get online with each.

# ind Optimizing the "Hub"

er WordPress self-hosted blogs for one very big reason: There
is you can download and install, that will enable all of the cool
ous section, like automatically tweeting your blog posts and
ocial media properties.

ss is that most hosting companies include it as part of their
e to do any setup. They'll take care of it.

o your new blog:

1. Register a domain name. Preferably it should be relevant to your business, or can be your own name (example: I own FrankRumbauskas.com). I recommend GoDaddy for both domain names and web hosting, due to the all-inclusive nature of their services, their reliability, and their extremely low cost. Prices are always subject to change, but at the time of this writing a domain name costs $10/year to register and own, and web hosting is only $5/month.

2. Once your domain name is registered, add the Economy Hosting option. This is the one costing $5/month as I write this, in 2012.

3. After this is all done, follow GoDaddy's instructions to install WordPress on your blog. I'm not going to go into details here, because they can change at any time, and because they make it so nice and easy and do it all for you.

Once this is all complete, the next step is to log into your new WordPress installation, install a theme, and optimize the blog for the search engines.

WordPress themes are what determine the look & feel of a site. The basic, pre-installed theme is just fine for our purposes. However, if you want to put a little bit of effort into it, you can very easily turn a basic WordPress installation into a pretty dazzling site. Just do a Google search for "wordpress themes" and begin shopping!

My favorite are the themes from StudioPress.com. In fact, one of my own blogs at www.nevercoldcall.com/blog is using the "Education" theme from StudioPress.

Take your time in browsing through available WordPress plugins, themes, widgets, and more - the possibilities are truly endless and you can customize to your heart's content. This part of the process - using your own creativity to customize your site - is beyond the scope of this book, so for now, I'm going to get into the "under the hood" technical instructions on optimizing the site so the search engines will love you.

Step 1: Go to the "Settings" menu and find "Permalinks." Click on it, choose the "Custom Structure" button, and type this into the field: /%postname%/

○Custom Structure            /%postname%/

Step 2*: Go to "Genesis" and then SEO settings. Rather than explain everything step-by-step, here is an image of how you'll want to set yours up:

## Doctitle Settings

*The Document Title is the single most important SEO tag in your document source. It succinctly informs search engines of what information is contained in the document. The doctitle changes from page to page, but these options will help you control what it looks by default.*

***By default,*** *the homepage doctitle will contain the site title, the single post and page doctitle will contain the post/page title, archive pages will contain the archive type, etc.*

☑ Append Site Description to Doctitle on homepage?

☐ Append Site Name to Doctitle on inner pages?

Doctitle ( `<title>` ) Append Location:
*Determines what side the appended doctitle text will go on.*

○ Left
◉ Right

Doctitle ( `<title>` ) Separator: [ — ]
*If the doctitle consists of two parts (Title & Appended Text), then the Doctitle Separator will go between them.*

## Homepage Settings

Which text would you like to be wrapped in `<h1>` tags?
*The* `<h1>` *tag is, arguably, the second most important SEO tag in the document source. Choose wisely.*

◉ Site Title
○ Site Description
○ Neither. I'll manually wrap my own text on the homepage

Home Doctitle:
[                                        ]
*If you leave the doctitle field blank, your site's title will be used instead.*

Home META Description:
[ Sales tips and advice from top sales professionals and sales superstars. Hundreds of articles on all sales topics here at The NeverColdCall.com Sales Blog. ]

*The META Description can be used to determine the text used under the title on search engine results pages.*

Home META Keywords (comma separated):
[                                        ]
*Keywords are generally ignored by Search Engines.*

**Homepage Robots Meta Tags:**

☐ Apply `noindex` to the homepage?
☐ Apply `nofollow` to the homepage?
☐ Apply `noarchive` to the homepage?

## Document Head Settings

*By default, WordPress places several tags in your document* `<head>` *. Most of these tags are completely unnecessary, and provide no SEO value whatsoever. They just make your site slower to load. Choose which tags you would like included in your document* `<head>` *. If you do not know what something is, leave it unchecked.*

**Relationship Link Tags:**

☐ Adjacent Posts `rel` link tags

**Windows Live Writer Support:**

☐ Include Windows Live Writer Support Tag?

**Shortlink Tag:**

☐ Include Shortlink tag?
*The shortlink tag might have some use for 3rd party service discoverability, but it has no SEO value whatsoever.*

Click "Save Settings" on the bottom, and you're done with that part.

Step 3: Again under the "Genesis" menu, go to "Theme Settings" and find Header Settings, Navigation Settings, and Breadcrumbs, about in the middle of the page, and set as follows:

---

**Header Settings**

Use for blog title/logo:  [ Dynamic text ‡ ]

---

**Navigation Settings**

**Primary Navigation**

☑ Include Primary Navigation Menu?

☐ Enable Fancy Dropdowns?

☐ Enable Extras on Right Side?

**Secondary Navigation**

☐ Include Secondary Navigation Menu?

*In order to use the navigation menus, you must build a custom menu, then assign it to the proper Menu Location.*

---

**Breadcrumbs**

**Enable on:**

☐ Front Page ☑ Posts ☑ Pages ☐ Archives ☐ 404 Page ☐ Attachment Page

*Breadcrumbs are a great way of letting your visitors find out where they are on your site with just a glance. You can enable/disable them on certain areas of your site.*

---

*Steps 2 & 3 are only applicable if you are using one of the Genesis themes from StudioPress.com, which I strongly recommend, but it's not a necessity. The free included theme, or any other WordPress theme, will work well for you.*

Step 4: Go to "Plugins," "Add New" and enter "WP to Twitter." Choose it in the results and follow the instructions to install it, then go into the plugin settings and follow the instructions to set it up and integrate it with your Twitter account. If you don't have a Twitter account, now would be a good time to go to Twitter.com and sign up.

Step 5: Go to "Plugins," "Add New" and enter "Google XML Sitemaps." Find it in the list and install it. Go into the plugin settings and click on the option to build the sitemap for the first time. This will hugely help your blog to rank well in Google search results.

Step 6: Think about what categories your posts will fall under. For example, on my blog, I have 'cold calling,' 'general sales advice,' 'sales closing,' 'referral selling,' among others. You don't need to do this right now - you can create new categories as you write new posts - but you'll definitely want posts under relevant categories, rather than leaving them as 'uncategorized' which is the default setting.

OPTIONAL: At this point you can browse through the thousands of free plugins that are available. In the name of saving you a lot of wasted time, here is a list that I recommend. I use these on my own blogs:

- Facebook Comments

- Fast Secure Contact Form

- FollowMe

- Jetpack by WordPress.com

- Shareaholic

- ShareThis

- Smart Youtube PRO

- WordPress Mobile Pack

I won't go into detail on what all of these do; you can do Google searches on them or look them up from within WordPress in the "Add New" section of Plugins. None are absolutely necessary, but all are beneficial to some degree.

Step 7: Create pages. Go to the "Pages" menu, "Add New," and add a few pages. At a minimum I'd have an "About" page, a page called "Products" or "Services" that details what you sell, and a "Contact" page. For your contact page, install the free "Fast Secure Contact Form" plugin and follow the instructions to add the form to your contact page and have the form submissions go directly to your email address. It's also a good idea to add your cell phone number, or any other contact information that will make it easier for prospects to reach you.

I also recommend putting some contact info, or links to your main or "money" website, on all pages. You can do this by creating a "Text" widget and putting it in the blog's main sidebar.

There is a tremendous amount of free information, tips, advice, suggestions, and more on how to get the most from your WordPress blog. Yoast.com is a good place to start. There are literally thousands of pages of information and free how-to articles and videos online, so I'm going to stop here; I simply want to make sure you have the necessities set up.

Your WordPress site is the hub of everything. This is where all the action happens. I'll now show you how to set up social media to be your automated promotion system for your site.

**NOTE ON TWITTER:** I personally have not found Twitter to be especially effective for salespeople, despite all the hype about it, so I'm not including a full chapter on it; however, it's fantastic for a local restaurants, retail stores, and small businesses to announce specials, promotions, and so on to their followers. If you fall into one of those categories, you should be using Twitter for those purposes.

# LinkedIn: The Social Media Goldmine

LinkedIn is my favorite social media property, for the reason that real, interpersonal networking happens here. While most other social media sites work on more of an automated basis - with exceptions of course such as direct messages on Twitter and Facebook - LinkedIn is all about reaching out to people, personally.

Having said that, it also gives you a tremendous amount of power and insight into actually finding those people. That's the real magic of LinkedIn.

In the "how to cold call if you have to" part of this course, I touched on using LinkedIn to make a roundabout sort of cold call to a prospective customer. In this chapter, I'm going to give you more specific tips on how to find and connect with the right prospects.

## Know Your Target Market

As I covered earlier in the course, you need to know the profile of your ideal prospect. This is even more important when prospecting on LinkedIn, because you're going to use many of these criteria as specific search items. Some of what you'll want to know in advance:

- What industries are they in?

- What about geographic location? Contacting people in a distant city does you no good if you can only sell within your own.

- How about job titles? Here's where you have to get creative and do a bit of brainstorming. If I want to connect with salespeople to sell my course, for example, I'd have to include the myriad of sales job titles that exist today: Sales rep, sales account manager, account executive, senior account rep, and so on and so on.

Once you have a good idea of the type of person you're looking for, you can begin searching LinkedIn to find these people.

Start by connecting with all of your current customers, something you should have been doing all along anyway. Begin by browsing around their networks. People hang out with their peers - so in the case of a decision maker, they're going to be friends and colleagues with people who are also decision makers at other companies. These are prime prospects.

Next, look in their "viewers of this profile also viewed" box. This is another great way to identify people who have a lot in common with your existing customers.

Next, look up what LinkedIn Groups they belong to, and begin joining those same groups. The nice thing about groups is that you suddenly have access to people who are not within your "three degrees," a restriction LinkedIn places on you in all other areas of the site, plus you can contact fellow group members directly, a nice advantage since many prime prospects will have direct messages disabled in their account.

Another creative way to use LinkedIn is to look up your existing customers, not as individuals but as companies. If your customers are larger and may have multiple locations or departments, you can find out who they are and who the decision makers are - then connect with them. This is a super easy way to make a sale, since the company itself is already a satisfied customer of yours and you're merely getting more locations on board with you.

## Network With Prospects and Customers

One of the most powerful ways to use LinkedIn, that almost no salespeople are doing, is to actively network with your customers and even with your prospects who haven't bought yet.

Remember that any and all businesses live and die by sales. This means that if you're in any kind of B2B sales, you are selling to people who are also selling. Maybe the specific decision maker you work with isn't in sales, but the fact of the matter is that their organization sells.

If you have small business owners among your prospects and customers, all the better, because many do all of their own selling, and if they don't, they're almost always directly involved with the company's sales process.

As you work LinkedIn - and your sales life in general - always keep your eyes and ears open for potential opportunities for you own prospects and customers. Sending them some business is a sure-fire way to gain their trust, make them like you, and obligate them to you. They're sure to reciprocate, whether that reciprocation comes in the form of direct sales from them, or in the form of referrals from them. Either way, you win, they win, and everyone is happy and prosperous in the end.

Of course, you have to make sure you work with them on the same level. Never act like a salesperson. Always act like a business equal. Walk the walk and talk the talk on the level of a business owner or executive, and they'll take you seriously.

## How To Work LinkedIn Groups

After you start joining LinkedIn groups where your ideal prospects hang out, don't rush to direct message all of them. In fact, don't direct message anyone yet, unless you really see a need to do so - such as a prospect who is actively in a buying mode for your product or service.

LinkedIn Groups are about building trust and relationships - and even more so as a salesperson, you're there to put your own credibility and expertise on display.

Scan the active discussions each day (I recommend receiving a list of discussions as a daily email, which you can set up in group settings). Look for discussions where you can contribute value, and do so. Just make sure you are giving real, valuable tips and advice, and not selling in the discussions. Actively trying to sell will not only undermine your credibility with prospective customers, but may get you banned from individual groups.

## Get LinkedIn Recommendations

One of the coolest features of LinkedIn is the Recommendations section. This is where actual customers can enter testimonials for you, and they will appear right on your LinkedIn profile!

Begin by contacting all of your existing customers - starting with your best customers first - and ask them to give you a recommendation on LinkedIn. LinkedIn does have a "Request Recommendation" feature, but don't use this until you've actually asked for it directly, whether that is on the phone, in person, or via an email.

Many busy people will ask you to write one for their approval. Don't be shy about this - it's common practice. Just make sure that what you write is accurate and reflects the experience the customer has had with you.

Also, before any recommendations go live on your profile, you'll have the ability to approve them. If any aren't quite what you were looking for, you can always ask the customer to edit it, or simply don't approve it and move on to the next one.

Finally, an easy way to get a recommendation is to first write one for the other person. This puts the law of reciprocity to work, and most people will be very happy to give you a glowing review after you've already given them one!

## Answer Questions

LinkedIn has a Questions section that works much like Yahoo Answers. Be sure you are qualified to answer the questions before you do so. And as always, give valuable and useful information. Be of service to others before thinking about trying to sell them anything.

In summary, you can see how and why LinkedIn is so powerful for salespeople. If you make the effort, you can probably get all the sales you'll need and more just via LinkedIn. Combined with the rest of this course, you'll be unstoppable!

One final note: There's no real need for you to use the Status Updates function. If you're following my social media strategy, you should have your Twitter feed auto-posting to that, so there's no need to do it manually.

# Facebook: Most Pages Suck. Yours Won't.

My Facebook strategy is two-fold:

1. In the "how to cold call, if you have to" section of this course, I showed you how to make inroads with highly desirable prospects by friending them on Facebook. So, for that reason, you'll want to have a personal Facebook account. If you'd rather not mix business and pleasure, set up a second one under a different email address. I know plenty of people who do this.

2. You'll also need a regular Facebook business page. Again, it's free, just Google "Facebook page" to find the "Create a Facebook Page" link. It should be first in Google results.

The next step is to integrate your Twitter account to auto-feed to your Facebook profile. Unfortunately, as of now, this is only possible with your regular Facebook account, and not with a business page. Simply search for "Twitter to Facebook," go to the page (make sure it's the real Twitter page on Facebook itself, and not a third-party service), and follow the very simple instructions.

That part is done!

As to the business page, that's more of a pain in the butt since you can't auto-feed to it. So, every time you create a new piece of content - and I do mean every time - you'll have to manually add it to your page. No big deal. It only takes a few seconds to copy & paste the link.

By *all* new content, I really mean each and every piece of content that you create: Blog posts, presentations, YouTube videos, press releases, articles about you or by you, and everything else you can think of. The purpose of the page is to share *all* of your content with the world, so use it!

## Building Facebook fans

I personally don't see a need to make a huge push to have thousands of Facebook fans - or "Likes" as they're now officially called - simply because I know plenty of people who do but who haven't been able to monetize it.

Having said that, there's value to getting people to "Like" you. Once they do, they'll receive every new piece of content that you post, right in their news feed. This is the real value of Facebook. It's sort of like the email newsletter list you're building: It's a way to "drip" content to prospective customers, in an unobtrusive way.

The most effective way to accomplish this is by having a "Reveal" tab on your page. You've probably seen these - there's a free download, or video, or some other piece of content that people want, but they have to first "Like" the page to see it.

You can use the exact same piece of content that you used when you created the email signup form on your personal website, per the instructions in that chapter of this course.

Creating the "Reveal" tab itself involves a bit of programming, and is beyond the scope of this course; however, there are tons and tons of services online that can do this for you at very low cost, so just search online for "custom Facebook pages", "Facebook reveal tabs," and similar searches to find them. You can also post a job at a site like Elance.com or Odesk.com to find an outsourcer to do it for you really inexpensively.

## Building an email list with Facebook

My favorite strategy is to have an email signup form right on your Facebook page, rather than a Reveal tab. You can designate this tab to be the default one that people who don't yet "Like" the page will see when they arrive. You can visit the Never Cold Call Again® Facebook page for an example:

http://www.facebook.com/pages/Never-Cold-Call-Again/255295034486523

The nice part about this is the Facebook iFrame feature, where you can actually have a real web page from your site display within your Facebook page. Again, the specifics are way beyond the scope of this course, and may change at any time, so I won't go into them here. The good news though is that it's a lot easier to do than building a Reveal tab, so if you're on a tight budget, look for some do-it-yourself instructions online. There are many out there.

## Contests

Once you have a nice fan base of a couple of hundred people or more, you can start doing fun stuff such as running contests. Both our local doggie day care where we take our Great Dane for boarding when we travel, and our baby photographer, do this on a regular basis. They'll run a contest such as, the person who "Likes" the highest number of items this week gets a coupon or some kind of small token prize.

There are ways to do this for free and there are automated scripts that you can use to run contests, such "Top Fans." Again, I'll leave it up to you to do your homework on Google and find the right solution for you.

The awesome thing about contests is this: Every time someone "Likes" something on your page, that fact is announced to the world in their own Facebook news feed. This creates a viral effect where others see it, will click on it, and may also become a fan of your page, and therefore automatically receive all of your new content.

This is doubly powerful because people tend to hang out with others like them. If your ideal prospect is a small business owner, for example, I can tell you that a huge percentage of their Facebook friends will also be small business owners, and will see all of the content that they "Like." So getting "Likes" is key - and contests are a great way to do it!

And so is great content. That's why it's so important to write blogs posts that are interesting, relevant, and useful to your ideal prospects. Be sure to post all of your content on your Facebook page, and you'll see that viral effect begin to happen very quickly.

# YouTube: Your Broadcasting Station to the World

Now we get into the fun part of the system: Syndicating your content all over the Internet, and the world!

The hub of your social media system is your WordPress blog, which feeds to Twitter via the "WP to Twitter" plugin, and your Twitter feed auto-posts to your LinkedIn and Facebook profiles. Brilliant - but you obviously can't pass text-only blog posts on to YouTube.

This is where you'll begin using your posts as transcripts for videos!

This is simple to do. Again, I won't give you any specific technical details about web video, cameras, and the like. But you do have a couple of options to work with:

1. Record directly from a webcam. If your computer has a webcam - and most do today - you can go to youtube.com/my_webcam and record a YouTube video directly from a webcam.

This is a nice option to use for the simple reason that you can use your computer screen as a teleprompter! Copy & paste your blog post or article to a NotePad or TextEdit document, position it high up on the screen so it's just below your camera, and you can use that to read the post directly into the camera, discreetly using your mouse to scroll down as you read.

2. Set up a regular camcorder. This is more time-consuming since you'll have to position a camera properly, will have to import the video to your computer, and won't have the benefit of using your computer screen as a teleprompter. But it's my preferred way to go. Even if it's something as simple as sitting at your desk as you shoot the video, you have more control over the look & feel and it will come across as a bit more professional and higher in quality than a webcam video.

Once you have completed and uploaded your videos to YouTube, post them on your WordPress blog, and on your Facebook fan page(s).

OPTIONAL: Third-party services such as TubeMogul are available to automatically upload your video to mass numbers of video websites. I personally don't do this because YouTube has the overwhelming share of traffic, but it's still an option nevertheless.

Another thing to keep in mind is the look & feel of your YouTube channel. You can customize a lot, and can link to each individual video so that it plays right on your branded channel's home page, which is a bit more effective from a sales & marketing viewpoint.

Another creative use of YouTube will be for uploading the presentations I'm going to discuss in an upcoming chapter. In getting the most from your blog posts and articles, I'm going to show you how to convert them to PowerPoint or Keynote presentations and upload them to presentation websites, which are hot right now in the business world. In addition to this, you can also record a voiceover on your presentations, save them as videos, and upload to YouTube and other video sites. Some of the presentation websites themselves even accept videos.

Remember, the central point of the Never Cold Call Again social media strategy is to take a simple, brief blog post, and get the most mileage out of it in terms of getting your content - and your name - spreading over as much of the Internet as possible! YouTube is not an end in itself, but rather another avenue to syndicate your content as a salesperson or small business owner.

# Podcasting: It's Already Done For You!

Podcasting is quickly growing in popularity, especially with the explosive growth of iPods, iPhones, and other podcast-compatible devices.

The good news for you is this: If you already have a YouTube video created, the work is done. iTunes and other podcasting engines are merely another place to upload your video - another avenue to get your content spreading like wildfire!

Here's how to get started creating your video podcast (sometimes called a vidcast):

1. Go to Feedburner (feedburner.google.com) and set up a free account. Go through the basic steps to enter your blog's name, URL, and other requested information.

2. Once your feed is set up, make a note of your feed's address. It's a good idea to email this to yourself or copy-and-paste it somewhere handy, since you'll need it again in a few minutes. Then, go to the "Optimize" tab in FeedBurner then click on "SmartCast" in the left-hand menu.

3. Click on the checkbox "Include iTunes podcasting elements" and choose the appropriate category and subcategory.

4. Enter a location for your iTunes Podcast image, that will appear in the iTunes store. You'll need to upload this to the web, where it's accessible. The simplest way is to upload it to your hosting account, or upload it to your blog, and then simply enter the URL to access the image here.

5. Complete the rest of the information such as podcast title and summary, and click on the "Include Media RSS..." checkbox on the bottom.

6. Finally, click "no" on "contains explicit content" and enter your name in the copyright & author boxes. Click "Save" on the bottom of the page when you're done.

The next thing you'll need to do is to upload your raw video - not the YouTube link - somewhere accessible on the web. You can upload the file to your web hosting account, or you can use a service like Amazon S3, my personal choice.

Once that's done, go ahead and post the link to the video on your WordPress blog. You have to have at least one live piece of content on the blog before setting up your podcast on iTunes.

Having done that, next, go into iTunes - you need to create an Apple Store account if you don't have one.

Go to iTunes store, then scroll to the very bottom and find Podcasts among the tiny links on the bottom of the page, and click on that. Next, find the Podcast Quick Links menu on the upper right of the screen and click on Submit a Podcast.

On this page, copy & paste your FeedBurner feed URL into the box. Click continue, complete all of the requested information, then submit it.

Then, wait anywhere from a couple of days to a week or more. Apple's approval times are very inconsistent and it all depends on how many others are in queue ahead of yours.

Sooner or later, you'll receive an email from Apple telling you that your podcast has been approved and is live on iTunes.

Congratulations!

This means that the initial video you posted the link to on WordPress is now live on iTunes. Have fun - subscribe to your podcast online, on your iPhone or iPod or other device, and show it off!

Going forward, you'll want to post that link to the raw video file right beneath the YouTube embedded video in your blog posts. They will feed to iTunes automatically via FeedBurner and you won't have to do anything at all. It's fully automated and hands-off.

HINT: If you're recording your videos directly on YouTube via a webcam, there's no raw video file to download. In that case, use the free tool at KeepVid.com which enables you to download the raw video version of any YouTube video.


## Create Your Second Podcast

Next, you're going to create another blog and another FeedBurner account to go with it.

Don't let this scare you - the good news is that it can be a very basic, plain-vanilla blog, and you don't have to do any of the work you did in setting up your first one!

My recommendation is Wordpress.com. It's their free, hosted blogging platform. Simply sign up, get a blog online, then set it up for podcasting in FeedBurner.

This time, you're going to do an MP3 blog. But there's more good news: You have already created the MP3 content and no further work is required on your part!

In order to get the MP3 files, simply use KeepVid.com to download an audio-only, MP3 version of each of your YouTube videos as you put them up.

Then, upload them and post the link to each in blog posts on your free Wordpress.com blog. FeedBurner will auto-feed these to your second, audio-only podcast.

So you get two podcasts, and double the exposure, and leads, for the price of one!

# The Untapped Goldmine: Document & Presentation Sites

One of the largest, untapped opportunities for salespeople online is with presentation and document websites.

These are sites that serve as libraries of PowerPoint presentations and PDF documents, and sometimes videos. And they represent your next step in automatically syndicating your blog posts as new content and getting more and more exposure and leads for yourself.

## Turn Blog Posts into Presentations

The first thing you need to do is put together a basic template in PowerPoint if you're on a PC, or Keynote if you're on a Mac. If you have both available, go with Keynote for sure. It is far more capable than PowerPoint and can create much nicer presentations. In fact it was Steve Jobs' own personal software that he used to create his famous Apple keynote presentations - hence the name - and finally one day he decided to make it available to the rest of us.

Once you have decided on a template, the next step is to take each new blog post as you write it, and convert it to a presentation. You do this essentially by taking each paragraph of your post and transferring the information to one or two slides, with the main points laid out as bullet points.

Or, if you're more advanced with PowerPoint or Keynote, you can get more creative with this. I have a freelancer who is an expert in PowerPoint who converts my articles and blog posts into stunning PowerPoint presentations for $20-30 each. You can view examples by going to SlideShare.net/nevercoldcallagain and you'll find my collection.

I found my PowerPoint expert on Elance.com. Odesk.com is another good source, as is Fiverr.com. Keep in mind that for the $20-30 per presentation that I pay, she does all the work of taking my blog posts, from scratch, and turning them into presentations. If you're willing to do a bit of work and create very basic, text-only presentations, you can have someone dress them up and make them look very professional for as little as $5 each.

Now that you've got your first presentation in hand, the next step is to get it online where people can find it! Here is a list of the best sites, with the most traffic, in order:

SlideShare.net
SlideBoom.com
AuthorStream.com
PowerShow.com
BrainShark.com

Register for a free account at each. Once that's done, upload your presentation to each one, complete with title, description, and keyword tags. Make sure you set them all to public viewing, so people can find them.

I get most of my traffic and views from SlideShare. In addition, every time I post there, I use their automatic "post to Twitter" and "post to Facebook" options, to spread the word.

You'll be quite surprised at the amount of traffic and views you can receive from these websites. They really are a very untapped goldmine of sales leads that few salespeople are using properly.

A final note on presentations: Customers love this stuff, so shoot an email off to your existing customers with a link to your presentation on SlideShare every time you do a new one. They'll forward them on to colleagues, meaning even more business for you! The same goes with prospects - it's another way to establish credibility and expert status with them.

## Presentation to YouTube

In the YouTube chapter I quickly mentioned that you can use presentation as YouTube videos. This is easily accomplished by recording a voiceover onto your presentations, turning them into videos, ready for upload to YouTube.

If you have a Mac, this is super simple since Keynote has a built-in recording feature. I'm not personally familiar with PowerPoint, but as always, there is a huge amount of free how-to information online about how to do this.

This is yet another way to get more & more mileage out of one little blog post!

## PDF Sites

The other big favorite of business decision makers are PDF document sites. Syndicating your content to these is super-simple because there's no conversion to do; you simply copy and paste your blog posts into Word or Pages documents, and save them as PDF.

For mine, I simply format them like a business letter. Nothing fancy, except for a logo on the top left corner of each page, and my name & contact info at the very beginning, and an "about" paragraph at the end, again with contact info. For examples, go to Scribd.com and search for my name.

With your PDF in hand, register for free to all of these sites:

Scribd.com
Docstoc.com*
Issuu.com
Calameo.com

*As a Mac user I have compatibility problems with Docstoc, even with Firefox and other non-Mac browsers, so if you're a fellow Mac user you may want to skip this one.

As with the presentation sites, upload your PDF to each of them, with titles, descriptions, and keyword tags. In creating these, be sure to use words that will get your content found by ideal prospects as they search the sites.

The more uploads, the better - this has a snowball effect. Block out regular time in your calendar each week for PDFs and presentation, as I do, and before you know it you'll have a ton uploaded and a ton of hot prospects contacting you!

# Your Social Media System of Systems

In summary, to make the most of social media, the key is to consistently generate new content on your blog, and then syndicate that content to as many social media properties as possible. Here's the checklist you'll want to use, each and every time:

1. Write a new blog post.

2. Via your "WP to Twitter" plugin, it will automatically tweet, and Twitter will automatically feed it to your personal Facebook page and your LinkedIn profile.

3. Manually post the link to the new article on your business Facebook page.

4. Post it as an article to EzineArticles.com, GoArticles.com, and other article directories.

5. Convert it to a press release: Free at PRLog.org, and, optionally, paid at PRWeb.com.

6. Copy & paste it into Word or Pages and save as a PDF document to upload to PDF sites.

7. Send a link to the PDF after you post it on Scribd, via Twitter.

8. Create a video using your article as a transcript and upload to YouTube, and, optionally, to TubeMogul.

9. Upload the raw source video file as a link on your blog, that you have set up to feed to an iTunes podcast.

10. Export the audio portion of your video, and upload it to your audio-only iTunes podcast.

11. Create a PowerPoint or Keynote presentation from the article and upload it to all of the presentation websites.

12. Send a link to your presentation on SlideShare, after you post it, via Twitter.

13. Post a link to your SlideShare presentation on your business Facebook page.

14. Record a voiceover on your presentation, save & export as a video, and then upload that as a second video to YouTube, and optionally to TubeMogul.

All of this content from ONE BLOG POST!

Hopefully now you can see why the usual approach to social media is completely ineffective. Most people think "social media" means sending out random tweets and posting news to their Facebook pages, but it is nothing of the sort.

"Content is king" is a phrase you'll want to remember always. Write it on a Post-It and stick it on your monitor. The key to success using the Internet and social media is to flood the net with as much content as possible.

Block out regular time on your calendar each week - say an hour each Tuesday and Thursday morning - and devote it to this content and social media strategy. In no time at all you will find yourself with tons of leads coming in, and eventually you'll even begin receiving invitations to post on high-traffic, high-profile blogs and websites as a guest author!

At that point, you'll be more than justified in demanding a raise or promotion!

## Part 5: The *Never Cold Call Again*® Referral Selling System

# Why Most Salespeople Fail
# At Referral Selling

One of the main problems with referral selling is what I talked about in the chapter on networking: Most salespeople try to find business at business networking mixers and leads clubs. The problem, of course, is that you're walking into a room full of salespeople who also need leads, and who therefore have absolutely nothing to offer you.

The other issue is that salespeople go about asking for referrals from customers, either old or new. This certainly isn't a bad idea, but it misses the lion's share of referral leads.

The lion's share comes from people of influence in your community.

In the chapter on appropriate dress, I told you to stop dressing like your customers, and start dressing like the people they turn to for advice.

Likewise, you need to start working on getting referrals, not from your customers, necessarily, but from the people they turn to for advice. These are the people who not only have the connections, but also have influence over your ideal target market, and who also trusted by them.

This strategy also puts leverage to work! Devoting your efforts to one small group of individuals who have influence over large numbers of prospects leverages your efforts in a huge way.

In this section of the course, I'm going to cover how to build a referral network from these influential people in your community, and I'm going to show you how to ask your own customers for referrals - properly.

# How To Find and Partner with
# The Hottest Lead Sources

## Who are the best referral partners?

That answer is easy: Influential people whom your ideal prospects turn to for advice.

When asked who prospects turn to for advice, the immediate answers most people give are the same: Accountants and attorneys, and they're right. But you need to get more specific than this. What kind of attorney? If you're in B2B sales, a divorce lawyer probably isn't your best bet, but a trademark or incorporation lawyer is going to be a hot target.

In addition, any type of small business that provides services will be a great source. Whether it's a B2B business that can refer you B2B sales, like a printer, or someone like a real estate agent who has a high volume of contact with B2C prospects, small business owners are fantastic.

Drilling down further, different types of contacts will have different intelligence. Printers can tell you who is expanding their advertising and marketing. Commercial real estate agents can tell you what companies are moving. Residential real estate agents can give you prime prospects for insurance. And on and on. (When I sold phone systems a long time ago, I got my best leads from commercial leasing agents.)

Going back to the chapter on free publicity, don't work reporters and writers just for publicity. Work with then on referrals. They are a great source.

If you're in B2C, think about luxury goods brokers to tell you who is spending money: Luxury car dealers, country clubs, and wedding planners, to name a few, are incredible lead sources.

Brainstorm and get creative. Accountants and attorneys may be the common answer, but they're just the tip of the iceberg.

## Leverage

The main advantage of building this type of referral network, of course, is that you won't have to cold call. But in addition, the power of leverage works for you in two big ways:

1. One good source can give you 30, 40, 50 sales, versus putting the same amount of effort into a low-return activity like leads clubs, or cold calling, and they'll close a lot faster

2. The quality of these leads will be far superior, and they'll generally be bigger deals than leads from other sources

## How to find hot referral sources

Most salespeople understand the concept of having powerful, influential people sending you leads, but don't know how to get there; in fact many have already tried and failed. The good news is that there is a systematic strategy I'm going to give you to come up with a solid list of referral sources, who you'll begin working in order to establish relationships with them and begin enjoying their hot referrals.

First, you have to understand the three categories of people you'll be working:

### 1. Your own influencers

These are the people that YOU turn to for advice and help! Some examples of those who you may already be a client of, and who are connected and influential in the community, might include your CPA, attorneys, doctors, dentist, veterinarian, real estate and insurance agents, chiropractor, masseuse, car wash, car dealer, your kids' coaches, and many more.

### 2. Your friends' influencers

Same as above, but this time it's the same list of people but for your spouse, parents, friends, and so on.

### 3. High-Value influencers

These are the ones who you don't know, they don't know you, but they're going to be the hottest lead sources, like the commercial leasing agents I worked with in selling phone system. A bit of good news: These people might be the highest value, but aren't necessarily the hardest to get to, for the reason that they don't know you and therefore don't hold any stereotypes about you. Using the instructions I'm going to give you, along with my previous advice on power and image, will get you in with them.

## Now For The Bad News

Now it's time for a reality check: Building your powerful referral network is the one area of sales where it really is a numbers game! Cold calling isn't, as I've explained, but here it is, and here's why:

These people are in high demand, and they know salespeople want to connect with them. As a result you need to stand out from the crowd and use the strategy I'm going to give you, but at the same time, remember that they don't need you. Unlike a prospect who you uncover with the Never Cold Call Again system, who really does need what you're selling, these influential people don't need you, and a few won't be interested, no matter what you do. So the more you can think of - and the more creative you can be in doing so - the more success you will have in building your network.

So with that, let's move on to the actual strategy for getting powerful people on board, and sending you hot leads!

# Building and Maintaining the Referral Partner Relationship

Starting out, you want a nice long list of target influencers. You know who yours are, you know of many who are your friends' or family's contacts, and finally you need to make that list of the so-called "unattainables."

The first thing you need to do is begin narrowing your list. You do this by segmenting out the very desirable people from those who aren't quite so desirable. For example, I mentioned that when I sold phone systems, commercial leasing agents were hot. So where people at the phone company itself, who could tell me who was moving or establishing new service, and therefore might need phones.

On the other end of the spectrum, my dentist certainly falls into the "default" list of potential contacts, but isn't going to have anywhere near as much desirable information as the people I mentioned above. While he may come up with a lead now and then due to the sheer volume of people he has as patients, it's not going to be as consistent and successful as the others. So prioritize your desired referral sources as such.

## The Contact System

Before you begin attempting to contact anyone, you need to set up a way to track the manner and frequency of contact. I recommend a simple spreadsheet in Excel or Numbers. That's how I track most of my sales & marketing efforts, and I recommend it. It will save a lot of wasted time trying to learn project management software, and it's more effective.

As to how to contact, phone calls and emails are best, and direct mail - an introductory letter - is worst, but is necessary from time to time, depending on who you're targeting.

You also need to be consistent with this! Just as I block out time on my calendar a few days a week to write new Sales Tips emails for my subscriber list, you need to block out time on a regular basis to work this system and build your referral network of influencers.

## Start With Your Immediate Influencers

As you might imagine, the people you already know are going to be the easiest to get on board, and the phone is quickest and most effective.

Simply give them a call, which they'll take because they know you, and cover the following steps:

1. Tell them you have some important news about your business

2. Tell them you respect and admire their success, or how they run their business, and that you'd really value their feedback

3. Schedule a time to meet in person (close)

That's it. Simple, and it'll be easy with people you already know.

## Move on to your Family & Friends' Influencers

This one isn't quite as easy, so you have to frame the call in such a way that there is a benefit for them. Here's how to handle this one:

1. Call and introduce yourself as a friend/brother/customer of whoever who recommended them

2. State that you're calling because the person who referred you said how happy they are with the product/service/etc and you'd like to learn more, as well as tell them a bit about yourself

3. Schedule a time to meet (close)

With this level of influencer, you can also try sending an email, or a direct message on LinkedIn, since they may be difficult to reach on the phone as they don't know you and may not take calls from strangers - I certainly don't and those who have reached me in this manner have done it with email first.

Another great idea, if your friend or relative is comfortable, is to make a live introduction. This will cut down the odds of phone tag - even though you're being referred by someone the influencer trusts, because he doesn't recognize your name when you call or leave messages, you may not get a call back. A live introduction, on the phone, will eliminate this. If it's a high-value influencer, consider having your friend or relative set up an in-person meeting (offering to buy lunch is best) in order to make the introduction.

## Handling Objections

What's key here is avoiding getting into your pitch about why you're really meeting with them, or to talk about what you sell. That is a deal-killer, especially with the friends & family category who may already be on guard as to what you really want from them.

If it does come up, frame your response in such a way that you position yourself as someone who can give THEM referrals - because it's true! Networking for referrals is a two-way street. If someone presses for a reason, or initially objects, tell them that so-and-so said they're a great provider of whatever it is that they do, and that you come across people all the time who ask you where to go or who to talk to.

Here's an example: Let's say you are in some type of B2B sales, and you're working the printer who does your dad's business cards. If he presses for a reason for the meeting, say, "All the time, clients ask me who is a good printer in town, and my father is very happy and spoke very highly of you so I'd like to come by and see your operation, and explore a mutually beneficial relationship."

At this point your prospective referral source will see YOU as a prospective referral source and will be more receptive to meeting. Just be sure to avoid talking about what you sell.

## The Meeting

The purpose of all this, of course, is to get an in-person meeting with your potential networking partner. Once that happens, you'll want to start out by exploring their business and asking about who their ideal client is; in other words, what you'll want to look for in keeping your eyes open for referrals for them.

Having done that, begin going into the value you can provide for their clients. For example, in my Google AdWords management business ([www.TheROITeam.com](www.TheROITeam.com)), nearly all new clients come to us by referral, from a handful of key referral partners of mine. They are people who get the question all the time: "Do you know anyone who can do paid search marketing?" Or, "Do you know anyone who can help market our business online?"

There will be a similar set of questions that define YOUR ideal prospect. So know what they are, and explain them to your prospective networking partner.

The key here is to remember that by being able to answer questions like that from their clients, and knowing that their clients are getting excellent service down the road from you, your networking partner is actually providing more value to their clients, thereby increasing their own value in clients' eyes, simply by referring people to you!

This is a lot bigger than it may seem at first, but by simply being able to tell someone where they can get something they need, they look like a genius. Napoleon Hill talked about this when he said, "Think about how you can bring producer and consumer together."

Another thing you'll want to consider going into the meeting is whether you want to offer referral fees, as I discussed in the chapter on Networking That Works. In some industries this is not even possible; for example, financial advisors cannot legally do this, and insurance agents can only pay referral fees to other licensed insurance agents.

When I sold phone systems, on the other hand, there were no rules, so I paid referral fees out of my own commissions. I can tell you that they keep referral partners VERY excited to continue sending you leads, so definitely consider it if it's legal for you to do so.

Leave a good supply of your business cards behind, so your new referral partner can give them to potential leads.


## After the Meeting

After you meet with your potential new referral partner, keep in touch and don't let the relationship die. Become friends. Schedule regular lunch or breakfast meetings, and don't talk business all the while. Talk to them about the things that interest them! I recommend reading the book "How to Talk to Anyone, Anytime, Anywhere" by Larry King to learn how to be a great conversationalist.

Over time you'll find that it's a small percentage of your network who send the most leads, the most consistently. Those are the relationships that will remain prosperous and grow, and may even become lifetime friendships.

Now that you're armed with this power networking strategy, never ever go to a "lead club" meeting again, where everyone sits around asking, "Got any leads this week?"

# My "Under The Radar" Advanced Referral Selling Strategy

A few months ago I was asked to speak to a small group of salespeople and executives, my favorite kind of speaking event since it's more of a roundtable setting, versus speaking from a seminar or convention stage where I have little or no audience interaction.

As always, someone asked me, "What is the best way to get referrals?"

Of course salespeople want referrals! Many consider them to be the best type of lead you can get. My friend Jeffrey Gitomer, in one of his presentations, says he'd take one referral over 100 cold calls. They're that much more effective.

I explained a strategy I learned a while back from another salesperson, which I call the "By Referral Only" method.

With this strategy, you have the words "Appointments By Referral Only" printed right on your business cards, along with other correspondence, such as letterhead, and of course in your email signature.

## Why This Works

Before getting into the psychology of why this is so effective, let me tell you the rest of the story about that roundtable meeting.

When I answered the question, and explained my "By Referral Only" method, someone said that's exactly what Bernie Madoff used to reel in his victims.

I couldn't believe it, so I went back to my office and looked it up, and, sure enough, it was true!

Having seen television shows like *American Greed*, about Ponzi schemes, I was always baffled about how the schemers were able to get people to hand over their entire life savings, sometimes millions of dollars, as was the case with Madoff's victims, over to a complete stranger.

Learning that schemers use the "By Referral Only" strategy went a long way toward answering that question.

## The Psychology of Exclusivity

The method works because people want whatever they can't have, or in this case, what they can't seem to have.

Anything that is seemingly unattainable, or in high demand by others, commands more attention and more respect. This is the basis of the term "social proof" that you hear many marketers talking about.

When a marketer like myself posts tons of customer referrals on my website, it's not so much to show people that my product is effective, but more to show that many, many others are buying it.

So-called "exclusive" neighborhoods command higher real estate prices, not necessarily because they're any better than the rest, but because of an image of unattainability that makes people want it more.

When a prospect comes across your name, or website, or blog, or social media page, and sees the words "Appointments By Referral Only," they will make a special effort to try and meet with you!

This really takes the psychology of exclusivity - which hurts cold callers and benefits salespeople who do not cold call - to an extreme level that will have highly qualified prospects clamoring for your attention.

## Success Begets Success

It's a known fact that success, or any image of prosperity, attracts favorable attention always. That's why I included the chapter on image, and dressing for success, since far too many salespeople fail in this respect.

Since you cannot make a personal appearance before each and every person in the world who might buy from you, this "By Referral Method" does it instead.

When people see that you work by referral only, they immediately assume that you are hugely successful - so successful, in fact, that you are turning people away.

That, in turn, makes them want to buy from you even more!

So begin using the "By Referral Only" method immediately. Print a second set of business cards with "Appointments By Referral Only" printed on them, and add it to your email signature and your website, blog, and social media pages.

## Part 6: Take Action Now!

# Knowledge, Mixed with Action, is POWER

*"The man of DECISION cannot be stopped!*
*The man of INDECISION cannot be started!*
*Take your own choice."*

*- Napoleon Hill*

Of all those dangerous half-truths out there, perhaps none is more dangerous than the idea that "knowledge is power."

In reality, knowledge is only *potential* power.

It becomes power when, and only when, it's combined with organized *action*.

You now have the knowledge required to not only succeed in sales, but to quickly rise to superstar levels, leaving your competition and your past far behind and reaching levels of attainment previously unimaginable to you.

Back in the days when I was struggling to make 50% of quota, I didn't think it was possible to make even 100% and keep my job for another month.

A few years later I was hitting numbers as high as 400% with ease, never working more than eight hours a day, let alone the ten or twelve hour days so many in our profession put in without anything to show for it.

I did it through the use of the knowledge I have shared with you in this book and that I now teach in my audio programs and live classes and seminars.

As I figured these things out through trial & error method, I sometimes failed to persistently keep the "action" part of the mix where it needed to be. I'd find something that worked, go out and close all the leads that came from it, and would be back at square one again.

You must not only put these programs into action, but you must be persistent and CONSISTENT with it. You must keep all your systems running all the time, forming one overall marketing system that will work, even when you're not, to keep you "fat and happy."


Here's a brief summary of all the knowledge and weapons you now have in your arsenal:

- **The ability to take back, and forever keep, your power**
- **An understanding of the supreme power of Image and the psychology of good clothes**
- **The ability to replace your limiting beliefs with positive, empowering beliefs and an understanding of why this works**
- **A working knowledge of the amazing power of Leverage and how to use and apply it**

- **Practical guidelines that, mixed with your own creativity, will allow you to create a super-powerful sales message**

- **Highly effective flyer distribution**

- **Correct and powerful ways to use the telephone**

- **How to use personalized email to your advantage**

- **A free newsletter giving your prospects useful, beneficial information that will forever obligate them to you**

- **Secrets of effective email marketing**

- **How to create your own very inexpensive website that acts like a giant net to "catch" leads and bring them in**

- **How to properly conduct free seminars that will educate your prospects in a way beneficial to them and provide you with ultra-high quality leads**

- **How to stop buying into the myth of "consultative selling" and become a true consultant to your prospects and customers**

- **How to speak your way to sales success**

- **A social media "system of systems" that will generate massive leads for you on autopilot**

- **The one approach to networking that really works in a big way**

- **A referral selling system that will guarantee so many leads, you'll never have to prospect again**

- **Getting free publicity that's worth more and is more effective than thousands of dollars in paid advertising**

That's quite a list.  It's all yours.  You have the knowledge, but only YOU can give yourself the power by putting that knowledge into ACTION!

The choice is now yours.  Do these things and reap untold sales success that you never even dreamed of.

### Don't Get Caught Up in "Time Management"

As you prepare to put the Never Cold Call Again® system into use, it's easy to get overwhelmed by the sheer amount of information and techniques it conveys, and, as a result, many readers get caught up in "time management."

The problem is that they end up wasting more time fussing with so-called time management systems than they ever did before!

I've tried a few popular time management systems myself, and software too. And I've never found anything that works better than this:
Each day I grab a Sharpie marker and a blank sheet of paper, I make a list of everything I need to do that day, and as I complete each item, I cross it off the list.

That's it. Simple!

The major problem with time management systems, and the reason I don't bother with them anymore, is because they over-complicate the issue to the point where you spend more time managing your time management system than you do getting any actual work done.

Having to categorize each "to-do" into different priorities, contexts, locations, and ever more rubbish is just a waste of time.

My advice is to just get to work, instead of figuring out how to schedule and prioritize your work.

Thank you for taking the time to read this, and for placing your trust and confidence in me and in this program.  In closing, I'd like to leave you with one final thought from Napoleon Hill, one that is so relevant to this subject of taking action:

### TIME!

Procrastination robs you of opportunity.  It is a significant fact that no great leader was ever known to procrastinate.   You are fortunate if AMBITION drives you into action, never permitting you to falter or turn back, once you have rendered a DECISION to go forward. Second by second, as the clock ticks off the distance TIME is running a race with YOU.  Delay means defeat, because no man may ever make up a second of lost TIME.  TIME is a master worker which heals the wounds of failure and disappointment and rights all wrongs and turns all mistakes into capital, but, it favors only those who kill off procrastination and remain in ACTION when decisions are to be made.

Life is a great checker-board.  The player opposite you is TIME.

If you hesitate you will be wiped off the board.  If you keep moving you may win.  The only real capital is TIME, but it is capital only when used.

You may be shocked if you keep accurate account of the TIME you waste in a single day.

. . . .

*Move by move Time has wiped off Mr. Average Man's men until he is finally cornered, where Time will get him, no matter which way he moves.  INDECISION has driven him into the corner.*

# "Stop Cold Calling and Start Selling" Quick-Start Exercises

*This document is composed of the following sections:*

1. How I know that cold calling doesn't work

2. An Explanation of Buying vs. Selling

3. Re-framing my limiting beliefs

4. How I intend to take back my power in selling situations

5. How I intend to power up my image

6. Filters and Amplifiers in my own selling

7. My sales message – the "ad content" I intend to use

8. My sales plan – including how I intend to use and apply each of the following:

   - Flyers
   - Powerful Phone Techniques
   - E-Mail, both personal and mass email
   - Your free newsletter
   - Your lead-generating website
   - Your seminar plan
   - How you can be a consultant
   - Effective networking
   - Your publicity plan
   - Your speaking plan
   - Your Social Media plan
   - Your Referral Selling plan

9. My Social Media plan

10. My Referral Selling plan

1. How I know that cold calling doesn't work

On a separate page, please write a paragraph or paragraphs describing the reasons why you believe cold calling does not work. Include any true stories or personal experiences you've had that may serve to justify your belief that cold calling doesn't work, or prove it through real-life experiences. If you still believe deep down that cold calling works or is necessary, this exercise will be a challenge for you and will help you to overcome that belief and open your mind to new ideas. We find this to be the case with many of our students.

2.  An explanation of buying vs. selling

On a separate page and in your own words, please write an explanation of the differences between buying and selling as they are defined in the book.  It is important for you to understand this core concept which forms one of the underlying principles of the program, and this exercise will help to solidify your understanding and acceptance of the principle.

3.  Re-framing your limiting beliefs

We all have limiting beliefs that hurt our chances for success, or, at the very least, prevent us from realizing our maximum potential.  Some examples of limiting beliefs and how to re-frame them in a positive manner are as follows:

"I can't afford it" can be reframed as "How can I afford it?"

"I can't do this" can be reframed as "How can I find a way to do this?"

"How can I overcome the fear of rejection" can be reframed into affirmations such as "I like hearing prospects say 'no' because it brings me closer to 'yes'" or "It doesn't matter whether or not they buy – I don't need their business and have plenty of other deals lined up."

"How can I avoid doing stupid things?" can be reframed into an affirmation such as "I'm a genius and only do brilliant things."

On a separate page, write out as many of your limiting beliefs as you can think of.  Be brutally honest here.  Once you've written them all out, write out re-frames for all of them.  These re-frames can be in the form of questions or in the form of affirmations.  In either case, be certain that your re-frames will feed your subconscious with only good, positive thoughts and ideas to work with.

*Once you've reframed your limiting beliefs, USE your reframes!  Memorize them and USE them whenever any of your limiting beliefs come into your mind!*

4.  How I intend to take back my power in selling situations

Write out situations in the past where you've given away some or all of your power to a prospect or customer.  Think of every possible scenario.  Then write out how you intend to handle those same types of situations in the future in a manner that KEEPS all of your power for YOU.  (This is very similar to the exercise on re-framing limiting beliefs – you're re-framing situations and changing them from situations that take your power to situations in which you KEEP your power.)

5.  How I intend to power up my image

Write a description of how you've typically dressed, conducted yourself, and presented yourself in selling situations.  Now take a look at it and think about it and think of ways that you can change certain things in a manner that will power up your image.  Remember that the key to successfully using the power of image is to realize that you must present yourself in the same manner as the people your prospects turn to for advice and to adopt their image as your own.  (Again, this can be seen as a re-frame.)

6.   Recognizing filters and amplifiers in my own selling

Review the chapter on Filters and Amplifiers. Keeping those definitions in mind, replay in your mind your typical sales situation and think of as many filters as you can. Apply this exercise to all stages of your selling, from pre-prospecting preparation all the way through to post-sale follow up. Identify as many filters as you possibly can and figure out how to eliminate them or convert them into amplifiers. Write those filters down on paper along with how you intend to change them into amplifiers.

7.   My sales message

Review the chapter entitled, "How to Succeed in Sales." Using those guidelines, write out your sales message. Be sure to apply all the guidelines given. Because your message will probably evolve over time or change with your product offerings, a 'rough draft' or outline is okay here.

8.   My sales plan

Write out a preliminary sales plan based upon the system taught in this program. Include a brief explanation of how you intend to apply each of the following: Flyers, telephone techniques, email, free newsletter, fax marketing, your own website, seminars, consultant, free publicity, networking/referrals. Include, if possible, a timeline, a flowchart, or a business plan, showing when each of these methods will be implemented, in what fashion, etc.

9. My Social Media plan

Begin at once to implement the Social Media system explained in this course. Start out by registering for any of the social media properties you're not currently registered with such as Twitter, Facebook (including the creation of a business page), and other listed. Then follow the instructions to create your Wordpress blog and configure it to feed to your Twitter, feed that to the various pages, and so on down the line. Be sure to use the checklist in the Social Media section to syndicate each new article or blog post you create across a wide variety of web properties, and commit to creating and syndicating no less than two new articles or posts each week. Regularly block out time on your calendar to do this.

10. My Referral Selling plan

Using the strategies explained, begin following the steps to build a powerful referral network full of influential referral partners, and begin building those relationships. Also order new business cards and update your email signature, websites, and pages as necessary to use the "By Referral Only" strategy.

# APPENDIX A - SHORTCUT TO SALES SUCCESS

Several months ago, I signed up for Simpleology: The Simple Science of Getting What You Want. It's a free online multimedia course, set of outstanding time-management tools, and lots of other things all wrapped up in one, run by #1 best-selling author Mark Joyner. You can learn more and register for free here:

<u>Simpleology.com</u>

I'm completely amazed at how much more productive and less stressed my life has become since starting Simpleology. I strongly recommend it to everyone, regardless of what your line of work may be. In fact, several weeks ago I had finished lots of traveling and came home to a massive amount of overdue work. I figured the stack on my desk would take three days to get through, but thanks to Simpleology's productivity tools I got through it in three hours! I highly recommend Simpleology to all salespeople.

Again, here's the link to sign up for this amazing, free tool:

<u>Simpleology.com</u>

# APPENDIX B - RECOMMENDED READING

The following books and authors have been very influential in my life and I highly recommend them not only for success in sales, but for success in life in general, both financially and otherwise.

The Law Of Success                                                    Napoleon Hill
(Over a thousand pages, but worth it. I read it continually.)

The Sales Bible                                                       Jeffrey Gitomer

Think and Grow Rich                                                   Napoleon Hill
(This is the 'lite' version of The Law of Success.)

Selling to VITO:  The Very Important Top Officer                      Anthony Parinello
(Excellent book on selling to C-Level executives.)

Little Red Book of Selling                                           Jeffrey Gitomer
(In my opinion, the best all-around sales book.)

How I Raised Myself from Failure to Success in Selling                Frank Bettger

The Irresistible Offer                                                Mark Joyner
(A marketing book that is very applicable to sales.)

Rich Dad's Cashflow Quadrant                                         Robert T. Kiyosaki
(Excellent book on the power of systems.)                            and Sharon L. Lechter

Retire Young, Retire Rich                                            Robert T. Kiyosaki
(Excellent book on the power of leverage.)                           and Sharon L. Lechter

The Science of Getting Rich                                          Wallace D. Wattles
(Incredible success book)

My Life and Work                                                     Henry Ford

Concentration                                                        Russell Conwell

## IMPORTANT – PLEASE READ!

COPYRIGHT INFORMATION
THIS PRODUCT AND ASSOCIATED MATERIALS ("PRODUCT") COPYRIGHT 2003-2013 BY FRANK J. RUMBAUSKAS, JR. AND FJR ADVISORS, INC., ALL RIGHTS RESERVED. FEDERAL COPYRIGHT LAW PROVIDES SEVERE CIVIL AND CRIMINAL PENALTIES FOR THE UNAUTHORIZED REPRODUCTION OR PUBLIC DISTRIBUTION OR EXHIBITION OF COPYRIGHTED MATERIALS. THIS PRODUCT IS PROTECTED BY TITLE 17, UNITED STATES CODE, INCLUDING BUT NOT LIMITED TO SECTIONS 501, 504 AND 506. THE STAFF OF FJR ADVISORS, INC. AND THEIR ATTORNEYS REGULARLY SEARCH THE INTERNET FOR UNAUTHORIZED DISTRIBUTION AND/OR DUPLICATION OF THIS PRODUCT.

TRADEMARK INFORMATION
"COLD CALLING IS A WASTE OF TIME: SALES SUCCESS IN THE INFORMATION AGE" AND "NEVER COLD CALL AGAIN" ARE REGISTERED TRADEMARKS OF FJR ADVISORS, INC. AND MAY NOT BE USED IN ANY FORM WITHOUT EXPRESS WRITTEN PERMISSION FROM FJR ADVISORS, INC. VIOLATORS WILL BE PROSECUTED TO THE FULLEST EXTENT OF THE LAW.

MATERIALS MAY NOT BE RESOLD
LICENSED ONLY FOR NON-COMMERCIAL PRIVATE EXHIBITION. ANY PUBLIC PERFORMANCE, OTHER USE, OR COPYING IS STRICTLY PROHIBITED. YOU ARE RECEIVING A SINGLE, NON-TRANSFERABLE, NON-ASSIGNABLE LICENSE FOR THE NON-COMMERCIAL PRIVATE USE OF THIS PRODUCT. THIS PRODUCT IS NOT TO BE RE-SOLD AT ANY TIME. IN OTHER WORDS, THESE MATERIALS ARE FOR YOUR OWN PERSONAL USE AND ARE NOT TO BE SOLD OR DISTRIBUTED TO OTHERS NOW OR AT ANY TIME IN THE FUTURE. THE AUTHOR AND FJR ADVISORS, Inc WILL, IN ALL CIRCUMSTANCES, PURSUE INFRINGERS FOR THE MAXIMUM REMEDIES, PROTECTIONS, AND STATUTORY DAMAGES ALLOWABLE UNDER TITLE 17, USC, CHAPTER 5.

DISCLAIMER AND RELEASE FROM LIABILITY
YOU UNDERSTAND THAT THE STATEMENTS MADE AND CONCEPTS CONVEYED THROUGHOUT THIS PRODUCT ARE A PERSONAL OPINION ONLY. THE AUTHOR AND FJR ADVISORS, INC. MAKE NO REPRESENTATION OTHERWISE. YOU ARE RESPONSIBLE FOR YOUR OWN BEHAVIOR AND CONDUCT. NONE OF THE MATERIAL CONTAINED HEREIN IS TO BE CONSIDERED LEGAL OR PERSONAL ADVICE. FJR ADVISORS, INC. MAKES NO WARRANTIES OF ANY KIND (EITHER EXPRESSED OR IMPLIED) AND YOU ALONE ASSUME ALL RISK ASSOCIATED WITH THE USE OF THIS PRODUCT. BY USE OF THIS PRODUCT, YOU WAIVE ANY CLAIM WHATSOEVER AND HOLD HARMLESS THE AUTHOR AND FJR ADVISORS, INC. AND ANY OF ITS OFFICERS, STAFF, ADVISORS, REPRESENTATIVES, CONTRACTORS OR DESIGNEES THAT MAY ARISE FROM SUCH USE. THIS WAIVER SPECIFICALLY INCLUDES ANY CLAIM ARISING FROM A PRODUCT AND/OR SERVICE WHICH YOU PURCHASE FROM FJR ADVISORS, INC. OR ANY INFORMATION YOU RECEIVE VIA POSTAL MAIL, E-MAIL, FAX, TELEPHONE, OR OTHERWISE. THIS INCLUDES RESPONSIBILITY FOR THE ACCURACY OR COMPLIANCE WITH ANY APPLICABLE LOCAL LAWS. FJR ADVISORS, INC. AND THE AUTHOR FRANK J. RUMBAUSKAS, JR. SHALL NOT BE LIABLE IN ANY WAY WHATSOEVER, INCLUDING BUT NOT LIMITED TO NEGLIGENCE, FOR ANY SPECIAL OR CONSEQUENTIAL DAMAGES RESULTING FROM EITHER YOUR USE OF THIS PRODUCT OR YOUR INABILITY TO USE IT. THIS LIMITATION INCLUDES ANY CIRCUMSTANCE IN WHICH FJR ADVISORS, INC. OR ANY OF ITS REPRESENTATIVES HAVE BEEN ADVISED OF POTENTIAL LIABILITY. CERTAIN APPLICABLE LAWS MAY NOT ALLOW ALL THE LIMITATIONS OF LIABILITY DESCRIBED HEREIN. YOU AGREE THAT FJR ADVISORS, INC.'S TOTAL LIABILITY TO YOU INCLUDING BUT NOT LIMITED TO LOSSES, DAMAGES, CAUSES OF ACTION, AND/OR NEGLIGENCE SHALL NOT EXCEED THE TOTAL MANUFACTURER'S SUGGESTED RETAIL PRICE OF THIS PRODUCT AT THE TIME OF PURCHASE.

RETURN POLICY

PLEASE SEE THE COMPLETE RETURN INSTRUCTIONS AT:

**www.nevercoldcall.com/return.htm**

OUR FRIENDLY AND COURTEOUS STAFF WILL PROCESS YOUR RETURN PROMPTLY, BUT RETURNS THAT DO NOT FOLLOW THE RETURN INSTRUCTIONS WILL NOT RECEIVE REFUNDS!